An Angelic Boy's Divine Assignment
and His Family's Story of Hope and Healing

Luca's Light

by Elena Giordano

Luca's Light
An Angelic Boy's Divine Assignment And His Family's Story of Hope and Healing
www.lucaslightbook.com

Published by The Core Media Group, Inc., www.thecoremediagroup.com

Cover Design: Emily Morelli & Nadia Guy
Interior Design: Nadia Guy

ISBN 978-1-950465-51-4

Printed in the United States of America.

Table of Contents

Each year, approximately 16,000 children are diagnosed with some form of cancer. Brain cancer recently replaced leukemia as the leading cause of cancer death among children.

We want to do everything we can to find a cure for this modern-day affliction. So please join us as we shine Luca's Light on the plight of pediatric brain cancer to raise awareness and find a cure for this deadly disease. The majority of proceeds from the sale of this book will go toward research for pediatric brain cancer.

This book is dedicated to our sweet Luca.

February 5, 2001-June 21, 2017

PROLOGUE

Road to Heaven

My son, Luca, was driving with his left wrist resting on the steering wheel. There were no scars on his head, and his hair was full. He no longer had the patches of baldness from endless rounds of chemotherapy and radiation. His right arm was draped over the back of the passenger seat where my sister and best friend, Christi, sat. They were in a classic red Cadillac convertible, the one with the big fins. The top was down, and Christi's long, red hair was blowing in the wind. They were a beautiful symbol of freedom.

Both Luca and Christi loved the road. Christi would always call me while she was driving. Living almost two thousand miles away from one another—I lived in Southern California, and she lived in Minnesota—the road was our time to connect. She had a two-and-a-half hour drive from Lake Shore, Minnesota, to Minneapolis for school, where she was getting her master's degree in psychology. She would call me a couple times a week. She was my rock, my saving grace, at a time when I felt like I was drowning, as I watched Luca endure the intensity of another cancer treatment and stood by his side as his primary caregiver.

Not only did Christi have a master's-level understanding of psychology, grief, and trauma; she also understood the darkness I was going through. She, too, wrestled with depression. I leaned on her in a way that I couldn't anyone else. My parents had named her Christina because it means "Christ in you." She reflected Christ to me because of her willingness to sit with me in the valley.

As for Luca, being in a classic car, on the road, in the front seat, next to someone whom he loved, was one of his happy places as well. The fact that he was driving an iconic Cadillac was fitting. Luca *loved* exotic cars. So does my husband, Frank. I think Luca's love for sports cars made Frank more willing to spend the money on them. When you raise a child with special needs, communication can sometimes be difficult. You try to connect with your child any way you can. The road was one of the places they could connect.

When Frank would get home from work, Luca would often hear the garage door, let out a squeal, and run out into the garage to greet his dad. They would go on an after-work drive, the top down, through the San Diego suburbs and hills. On one of their outings when Frank took Luca and Gabriel, Luca's brother, on a drive, a police officer pulled them over. The officer caught them jumping off the line at a red light just as the cop was—I kid you not—leaving a doughnut shop. Those Giordano boys—always getting in some kind of trouble!

Anyway, I think often about Luca driving Christi around in that red Cadillac convertible. I wonder where they were off to. I wonder what they were talking about. I wonder what music they were listening to.

My mom was the one who had such a vivid dream. As she shared the scene with me, her eyes welled up. It was as if she had caught a glimpse into another realm. Both Luca and Christi were finally free from their pain, on those heaven-soaked open roads, enjoying one another's company without time ticking down.

A peace washed over me. But so did pain and tears. I missed them.

My phone rang at three thirty in the morning.

I wish I could say I was in the middle of a good night's sleep, but it had been a long day. Luca, sixteen years old at that time, was in the middle of his third bout with brain cancer, and he was in enormous pain. The medication from the chemotherapy had crushing side effects. I had never seen him so weak, so utterly removed from this life. I honestly thought we might lose him any day. All at once, his circumstance was terrifying, heartbreaking, unthinkable, and unbearable.

Life had already been difficult for Luca. He was diagnosed at age two with a serious form of brain cancer, and we had no choice but to send our son into surgery, chemotherapy, and radiation if we wanted him to live. As a nutritionist and holistic healing advocate, I found this a tough pill to swallow. Treatment ultimately saved his life at the tender age of two, but the extreme nature of the surgery, coupled with the intensity of chemo and radiation, left him with lasting brain damage. Luca grew up never knowing what it was like to be "normal." A true little warrior, he conquered brain cancer *again* at age four. And now, here he was, fighting for his life once more at sixteen.

When I got that call in the middle of the night, I knew it was bad. Does your heart ever sink into the pit of your stomach when you receive a call? Intuitively, I knew something was wrong.

I picked up the phone. My world collapsed on itself as I listened to the person on the line say that Christi—my sister, my best friend—had taken her own life on a camping trip near a Minnesota lake.

It's hard to go back and recall what happened next for me—to somehow dissect the pain and confusion of a panic attack. But Frank, my husband, would later tell me that I, for some reason, after a period of shock, ran outside, as if to confront God Himself in the stars, and collapsed on the front porch. My body was shaking. My soul ached. I felt like I was living a nightmare. Frank later told me I was screaming about how my sister was gone and how Luca would soon be gone, as well.

All I can say is that I felt like I couldn't go on.

But life somehow got worse. There's a cliché that says God never gives you more than you can handle, but I know through experience this isn't true.

The next day, while Luca was using the bathroom, he had a seizure for the first time in his life. I immediately yelled for Frank, and he helped me get Luca stabilized. We called 911, and thankfully, the paramedics arrived four minutes later. Their lightning-fast response might have saved his life. They observed the state Luca was in and suggested that we send him in the ambulance to Rady Children's Hospital, where Luca's cancer treatments had unfolded. Frank went with Luca in the ambulance, and I stayed at home with our other two children, Grace (thirteen) and Gabriel (nine).

It was as if life as we knew it was falling apart with each passing hour. Why was this happening?

As the ambulance pulled away, I stood in the driveway, where I had my emotional breakdown early that same morning, wondering if I had just said my final words to my son.

During the thirty-five-minute ambulance ride, Luca had four more seizures.

Luca had been diagnosed with brain cancer for the *third* time six months before. Since then, we had held onto the hope that God would miraculously heal our little Luca—that our testimony as a family would be one that might exemplify God's power, majesty, and healing. Though it was hard to own it in the middle of the third cancer battle, that was already our testimony to give. By age four, Luca had already defeated brain cancer against all medical odds—not just once, but twice. We had already experienced the miraculous gift of more than a decade of his presence. We understood just how serious the third cancer battle was, but deep down, we felt as if God would always allow Luca to somehow, some way, conquer whatever worldly challenge he faced.

But in those weeks after Luca's string of seizures, he continued to decline steadily.

I remember once asking Luca's doctor at Rady's what the signs would be if Luca's health were fading. Because of Luca's special needs and limited vocabulary, he had challenges communicating with us through words. He primarily spoke to us through emotion, which was often difficult to decipher. In complicated situations like this, it was impossible to have a full understanding of how he was feeling. The doctor told us that if he were nearing the end, his body would become extremely fatigued, and he would sleep.

As Luca's third cancer battle stretched past half a year, we began to see the signs. He was weak and began sleeping throughout the day. I struggled to accept the inevitable. First Christi. Now this. Where was God? In the midst of all this loss and grief, my own struggles intensified with soul-crushing weight. Beneath the loss and the grief that seemed without end, I became aware of a terrible sense of loneliness. On a deep level, I felt spiritually abandoned. I felt supernaturally alone, now without my Christi to lean on, and abandoned even by God. Looking back on how unbearable my life felt in that season, I am glad to have survived it at all. I call it "my dark night of the soul."

In the dark night of the soul, beneath the loss and the grief, there is sometimes a level of spiritual distress that shakes the very core of a person's foundation. Of course I was surrounded by loved ones who cared deeply about me, like my husband, Frank; my family; and my dear friends at church, but the person who was most aware of the details of my inner landscape—my depression, my anxiety, my insomnia—was now gone at a time when all these were at their peak.

Christi had attempted to take her life two times before that night at the Minnesota campground. Cancer had threatened to take Luca's life two times before, and now it looked like *his* battle, too, would be coming to an end. We had prayed fervently, diligently over the years for Christi's healing, for Luca's healing—why was God silent? I identified with Jesus's cry on the cross: "My God, my God, why have you forsaken me?" It felt like God had turned his back.

During this disorienting time, I found myself angry at God. I remember once praying, "At least your Son only had to suffer for a single day." I was referring to Jesus's crucifixion. That might seem sacrilege to put in a book, but isn't prayer, above all else, sincerity? Of course I knew Jesus suffered more than that—the anguish of sweating drops of blood in the Garden of Gethsemane on the eve of his arrest, the betrayal by his friends and closest followers, the public humiliation he experienced, and how he continues to suffer with us, in us, and through us today. But as a parent, your child's suffering can feel like something of a crucifixion. I felt like I could begin to relate to Mary on that horrific Good Friday, as she stared up at her mangled son on the cross.

I had watched Luca fight brain cancer at two years old, at four years old, and now again at sixteen. Less than *1 percent* of people are likely to get brain cancer. My son not only had significant special needs—which I imagine would be confusing enough for a young soul, unable to do what everyone else around him is doing—but we had also seen him diagnosed with brain cancer multiple times. Every passing day was filled with anguish and despair.

I was unable to attend the funeral of my only sibling and best friend because of Luca's dire state. Our family watched it remotely instead, cuddled and crying on the couch in the family room. We could tell that Luca was nearing the end of his life because he was spending more time sleeping and had very little appetite. I had no desire to leave his side except to take care of my basic needs or take a quick walk to the end of the street and back to try to clear my head. We had personally experienced God's miracles in the past, and we hoped and prayed with everything we had for just one more.

Then came that fateful evening on June 21, 2017. It was nearly two months after Christi's death on April 23—one day after my birthday—when Luca took his final breaths in our living room.

Sixteen years before, I had carried him in my body and watched him come into the world, and now, I watched him leave the world as he rested on my chest. As traumatic as it was, I did not want to let go. As I held him, though I was crying, I also could not help but think about how he was meeting Jesus for the first time.

Soon, as my mom would tell me weeks later following a vivid dream she had, he'd be driving Christi around those winding heavenly roads in a red Cadillac. Completely healed. Completely free.

Introduction

John Alessi wrote a beautiful story called *The Brave Little Soul* about a young soul in heaven who confronts God about the existence of suffering on Earth. God, though He did not design suffering, tells the soul that suffering has a way of connecting people with one another and unlocking a deep kind of love that can heal the world. Compelled by this mystery, the little soul says to God, "I am brave; let me go! I would like to go into the world and suffer so that I can unlock the goodness and love in people's hearts! I want to create that miracle!"[1]

The brave little soul came to Earth, suffered, and helped unlock the goodness and love in people's hearts. The story concludes: "The world was a better place. The miracle had happened."[2]

There is an angelic dimension of the brave little soul's life. Like an angel sent down by God for a purpose, the brave little soul was sent down by God to unlock goodness and love. And, like an angel, it then returned to its source in God the Father in heaven. Isn't that the spiritual trajectory for each of us if we choose to partner with God in our lives? We were chosen before the foundation of the world (see Ephesians 1:4), knit together in our mothers' wombs (see Psalm 139:13–14), sent forth into the world to love God and others (see Matthew 22:36–40), and we will eventually die and return to the God who crafted our very

1. John Alessi, *The Brave Little Soul* (independently published through CreateSpace, 2016).
2. Ibid.

being and existence (see Ecclesiastes 3:1—2). No, we are not angels, but we are spiritual beings. We are souls with divine missions to make the world a better place.

The Bible is filled with mysterious references to angels and their missions. There is the angel, Gabriel, who comforted Mary and Joseph when the Holy Spirit conceived within her a child. There is the angel who helped Moses lead the Israelites away from captivity as Pharaoh and his men chased them on chariots. There is the angel who wrestled Jacob throughout the night as he contemplated his life. There is Gabriel, again visiting the shepherds as they tended to their flocks, announcing to them the birth of a Savior in Bethlehem. There is the angel who visited Hagar when she and Ishmael were banished into the wilderness and dying of thirst. And there were the two angels who greeted the visiting women at Jesus's empty tomb and announced to them that Christ had risen.

Of course, there are many other biblical examples of angels. In these stories of angels and their missions for humanity, we are again reminded of the depth of our Father's love. We are also invited to, like the brave little soul, embark on our own spiritual missions: to allow God to send us deeper into our own lives to unlock goodness and love in people's hearts and to see how other souls around us are awakening more goodness and love in our own lives.

No wonder I call my son, Luca, "Angel Boy." The word "angel" in our common vernacular has less of a theological meaning and is used more to describe someone who has left a loving, heavenly imprint on our hearts and minds, someone who lights up our lives and shows us the way. During the most painful years of my life—and still to this day—God has shown me the way through the darkness of the valley with the guiding light of my special-needs son, Luca Giordano. He's been my godsend, my angel, my light. No matter how seemingly hopeless my situation, no matter how painful my circumstance, no matter how dark my life, there was always a light, somewhere, somehow, shining through Luca's eyes.

In the Bible, angels seem to show up during hopeless or unpredictable times. They light up the sky on an unassuming night or the tomb as loved ones grieve. When someone comes along at the perfect time and shows us the way, providing us a light in the darkness, I believe they reflect the heavenly missions of angels. Maybe it's a family member during a difficult time...or a friend during a period of transition...or a spiritual mentor during a phase of questioning...or a therapist when you felt like everything was falling apart. These people are heavenly godsends in our world that is marred with pain and suffering.

Life will get difficult. This is a given. Sometimes the darkness of this world can feel overbearing. Since those traumatic years, I've wrestled with depression, anxiety, and, perhaps worst of all, sleeplessness. But I also cannot take my eyes off the light. A light that was shining from perhaps the most unassuming places. Life seems to work that way, doesn't it?

In Psalm 23:4, the psalmist talks about walking through the valley of the shadow of death. Life requires a lot of us, and one of those requirements is going through the darkness. There is no dodging it. As the famous children's song says, "We can't go over it, we can't go under it, we have to go through it!" And, as the first chapter of John's gospel reads, the light always shines through the darkness, "and the darkness has not overcome it." Even if it's sometimes a faint spark in the distance, it's up to us to dare to see it...to find the courage to follow it...to trust it, even if that means venturing deeper into the dark.

It seems to me that the valleys of our lives come in three primary forms. You'll notice that each chapter of this book addresses all three of these levels in some way, whether it is an external or internal valley. Here are the three valleys:

- When life blindsides us and we are thrown into the valley (trauma or transition)
- When life demands that we make the long journey through the valley (the fight)
- When we have to surrender and heal from what occurred in the valley (grief)

My sweet Luca has been the divine spark in my life that has shown me the way. Toward something of healing, freedom, and wholeness in Christ, even in this fallen and broken world that has left wounds in my life that won't ever *fully* heal on this side of heaven.

This book might come across as raw and overwhelming at times. This is intentional, as the pain in the valley is real and should not be sugar-coated. That said, we believe you will be touched and inspired, especially if you have a child who is battling cancer—the most common cause of death by disease for children and adolescents in America.

Children are our angels in the sense that they are mysteriously sent directly from God to us. They become our teachers and guides. They help us to refine our spiritual seeing. They help bring us back to God and to our true selves. Luca was notably unique as a spiritual guide. He was specially gifted from the brain damage he suffered from the high-powered chemo treatments, which left him unable to formulate most words, eat normally, or have the independence of a child his age, but it made his love and joyful attitude especially profound. Battling brain cancer three times made his courage especially contagious. Luca, with his supernatural gifts of courage and hope, can help each of us see this world through spiritual glasses.

I believe the lessons he has taught me will help liberate you in some way, to venture *through* your suffering, and to live a more meaningful and abundant life.

Our lives are filled with the presence of angels. Whether we see them, or learn from them, is up to us.

This is what my angel has taught me…

CHAPTER 1

An Angel's Courage

Each child is a blessing from God. *All* of life is precious, no matter what our society says. There is no such thing as a child who does not bear the divine image; therefore, each child has something to teach the world about God—about what it means to love and be loved. Look into the eyes of a child, and you might see the Imago Dei—the image of God—staring back at you. Parents and grandparents know this to be true. Each child teaches us life lessons we could never learn on our own. The love we felt for our little Luca was infinite, and I imagine that's the way God must love us.

I believe that children with special needs and children who are battling the unthinkable cancer fight have so much to teach us about God, this world, and ourselves. These children are angels among us, sent by God, to a world He loves.

I still feel Luca's guidance today, through memories and stories. Each one of us carries stories in our bodies—the stories we tell ourselves and the stories of others' lives who have impacted us—and through his soul and spirit, which are not trapped in time. Angels leave an imprint on our hearts and minds that help us to keep going through life's confusion and difficulties.

Our "Mary and Joseph Moment"

In Scripture, this is most evident to me in the Christmas story, when Mary and Joseph find themselves in strange, incomprehensible circumstances. We read that Mary—a virgin betrothed to Joseph—is pregnant, her child conceived by the Holy Spirit. Can you imagine? Not only would this be disarming on every level—spiritual, emotional, mental, and, of course, physical—it would also have severe cultural implications. She could be put to death for getting pregnant out of wedlock. And Joseph, betrothed to Mary, could legally put her to death. An honorable man who did not want to see her physically harmed, his plan instead was to divorce her quietly.

But an angel appears to each of them and encourages them to stay the course. We read in the first chapter of Luke that Gabriel appears to Mary and says, "Do not be afraid, Mary; you have found favor with God. You will conceive and give birth to a son, and you are to call him Jesus…"

Mary humbly declares, "I am the Lord's servant. May your word to me be fulfilled."

We read in the first chapter of Matthew that an angel also appears to Joseph and says, "Joseph son of David, do not be afraid to take Mary home as your wife, because what is conceived in her is from the Holy Spirit…The virgin will conceive and give birth to a son, and they will call him Immanuel" (Matt. 1:20, 23). Joseph, too, humbly does what the angel suggests.

They were virtuous Jews who lived by the book, but they suddenly found themselves in a messy, taboo situation they never expected. Their lives changed in a heartbeat. Their hopes and dreams were instantly reconfigured. But the angel that appeared to each of them let them know they were not alone, informed them they were on a divine mission, and encouraged them to press forward in faith.

Mary and Joseph gained courage in the unknown from their faith and hope in God. They could not even grasp the full scope of whom their son, Jesus, would become. But they kept going anyway and trusted that something miraculous was happening beneath the surface, even if it meant a more difficult life for them in the shadows. They clung to God's promises that were delivered to them in their dreams by angels. In doing so, they provided a loving home for the Messiah of the world.

To a certain extent, Mary and Joseph's journey symbolizes each of our journeys. Each of us, in some way, is forced to cope with circumstances in life that we did not expect. Our hopes and dreams can change in an instant—with a phone call, at a traffic light, in a cancer diagnosis. Suddenly, our lives look nothing like what we had envisioned for ourselves. Yet we are challenged to press forward in faith, strengthened by our memories or experiences with angels.

As Mary and Joseph traveled to Bethlehem, they couldn't have possibly imagined the full scope of whom the baby boy resting in her womb would grow up to become. Truth is, no parent knows who their baby will grow up to become or the kind of pain and hardships they'll face in life. Just as Mary never could have imagined her baby boy one day being brutally crucified, no parent envisions their child having brain cancer or lifelong brain damage. Yet we are challenged to keep going, even in our unknowing, and to humbly adopt what Mary said as our own creed: "I am the Lord's servant. May your word to me be fulfilled."

Brain cancer was the last thing on my mind when Frank and I found out merely five months into our marriage that I was pregnant—we were thrilled and surprised, suddenly eager to become parents. Brain cancer was the last thing on my mind in my third trimester when Frank and I sat in an Italian restaurant and discussed what name we should give our son—we agreed on Luca, which means "Luke" in Italian, and it is the name of the author of our favorite Gospel.

It was the last thing on my mind when we welcomed Luca Joseph Giordano into the world on February 5, 2001, the happiest day of our lives—he weighed 7 pounds, 7 ounces, and measured 20.75 inches long. In other words, perfectly normal. It was the last thing on our minds when we held him in the stained-glass sanctuary of St. Therese's, when he was dressed in his head-to-toe white christening gown for Father Jack Cuddigan to sprinkle holy water on his forehead and baptize him in the name of the Father, the Son, and the Holy Spirit.

It was the last thing on our minds when we took him to his first San Diego Padres game that summer. Or when I wrote this in his baby book: "Our dream for Luca is that he will always be happy and successful in what he encounters. Luca has a personality all his own. He is very expressive, very strong, and has a high voice. Maybe he'll be able to sing well. We pray that Luca will know for himself beyond anything else that Christ is his Lord and Savior."

We couldn't imagine the full scope of what was to come. But the first sign was when we took Luca to Rome to meet Frank's extended family in Italy and Luca's great-grandfather, Nonno Beppe, burst into our bedroom, flipped on the ceiling light, and announced, "*Luca—c'è qualcosa che non va. È malato, di sicuro."*

Luca—something's not right. He's sick, for sure.

We thought the man was just old and crazy. It wasn't until Luca's weight dropped several months later and he began vomiting nonstop one day that doctors suggested that we get Luca a CT scan to make sure he did not have a tumor. The scan revealed a large mass on his brain. And that was when we first heard the word *medulloblastoma*, when brain cancer first crossed our minds.

This was our "Mary and Joseph moment," when we suddenly realized that our parenting journey was not unfolding how we expected it to unfold. Little did we know at the time that the proverbial angel who would visit us in our confusion and despair would come in the form of our very own son.

Angels inspire us to keep going—to, as the apostle Paul wrote in Philippians 3:14, "press on toward the goal to win the prize for which God has called me heavenward in Christ Jesus." We are challenged to make a home for God through the lives we live. We are challenged to believe and to trust what the angels in our lives have taught us so we can keep going in faith.

Not a day goes by that I don't think of Luca, and this is a good thing—not a bad thing! What Luca unlocked within me still helps me move forward through life's valleys. I hope Luca's story does the same for you. I hope that by sharing these stories about who Luca was—and what he taught us—they will help guide you on your spiritual journey, even when it's through the valley. I hope they'll help you find a light, focus on the light, and follow the light in the darkness. I hope they'll inspire you to keep going.

Keep Going when Blindsided by the Valley

So, who was Luca Giordano?

If you were to find a picture of him in our house, you'd see a beautiful face framed by a halo of soft brown hair accented with a touch of strawberry blond. His most striking physical features were his alabaster skin and piercing blue-green eyes that were the color of aquamarine stones. We had the same skin tone, eye color, and red in our hair. I often called him my Mini Me.

I say his eyes were piercing because when we looked into them, it was as if we were gazing into a heavenly portal. They were like hopeful beams of light. Those eyes had seen more suffering in life than one could ever begin to imagine for a boy his age, yet they never appeared strained, dark, hopeless, or even fatigued. His eyes always seemed to smile back at us. They radiated joy and reflected back an innocence that made us, too, begin to resurrect a childlike faith from our dreary souls. I would often catch myself staring into them with awe and wonder. They always seemed to rescue me momentarily from my own pain.

In a life filled with unknowing, transition, and loss, gazing on divine beauty—the Imago Dei—will do that to you. It's a rescue in the storm. Luca was my rescue.

I admit, those eyes sometimes also glowed with a sense of mischief and playfulness. It was often difficult to know what he was thinking or feeling because his vocal responses were sporadic and limited due to the brain damage he suffered when he was two. But he would often smirk and giggle when he saw or heard something funny, as his eyes wandered down to the floor. You could tell he was thinking about something hilarious, just unable to express it. I think he was an instigator, in his own way. He would play bizarre pranks on his siblings, Grace and Gabriel, like putting soggy potato chips—wet with *slobber*—back in the chip bag for them to find. They were disgusted, and understandably so, but I couldn't help but laugh. It was his way of messing with them.

To me, it felt like Luca believed he had a front-row seat to this thing called life. He was truly amused by people's behavior. He would watch in amazement whenever his sister and brother fought with one another, sometimes laughing and squealing in enjoyment. He would also listen curiously to our conversations at the dinner table, especially whenever there were any outbursts or rises in emotion. Sometimes he shot us a wild look, as if to say, "You people are insane!" His amusement led us to believe that he not only understood what was going on but could also see our trivial concerns for what they were.

He might not have been able to communicate verbally in-depth, but as any parent with a special-needs child will tell you, children who are challenged in this way often have a certain brilliance about them—a way of communicating something spiritual and true that goes deeper than words could ever go. They have a unique ability to transcend the worldly problems that eat at us and simply see them as they are. They are all about loving and blessing those around them, the very crux of the Gospel. You simply must listen with your heart, not just your ears.

Luca always let his heart lead the way, and it taught me the meaning of compassion. We learn compassion when we endure pain and loss. It opens us up to helping others in a more meaningful capacity through a newfound ability to sympathize. Compassion is similar to empathy, yet a little different. True compassion involves a personal level of suffering because others are suffering; you can't be truly okay until the person you love is okay. As American writer and theologian Frederick Buechner writes, "Compassion is sometimes the fatal capacity for feeling what it is like to live inside somebody else's skin. It is the knowledge that there can never really be any peace and joy for me until there is peace and joy finally for you, too."

In our culture, it's easier sometimes to just remain in our heads. But Luca didn't have that luxury. His heart was the main gift God gave him, and it had a way of touching everyone he interacted with. He may not have been able to have a political debate, discuss theology, or argue Christian apologetics, but people felt loved, understood, and accepted by him because of the way his heart shined.

I'm still learning from him, years after I kissed him for the last time. There have been days recently that I've really struggled and found it difficult to uncover joy. But If I can remember how he experienced joy, no matter what his situation was, it's a little easier, a little more accessible. The two words that describe Luca's personality the best are "joyful" and "determined." Though his life was filled with a great deal of pain and suffering, he could always rescue us with his laugh, smile, or childlike amusement.

His determination was not only evident in how he courageously fought brain cancer repeatedly; it also showed in his routines and obsessions.

For example,, he always wore a nose strip (which helped him breathe better while sleeping) and socks to bed, but if he didn't have socks on his feet, he would point at his nose or his feet, as if to say, "C'mon now, what are you doing?" His after-school routine as a teenager was similar. After I helped him wash his hands, he'd go straight to the pantry, retrieve a bag of chips, and head straight to the same spot on the couch every time. He'd then pick up his iPad and watch *Ratatouille* or *Megamind* or listen to music. He would watch specific scenes from these two movies over and over again, almost like a coach watching game film. One of his favorite songs was "God Gave Me You" by Blake Shelton.

Every time I heard Luca play it, I felt like I should be singing that song to him because God had gifted him to me.

In my own battles, I have often contemplated Luca's joyful and determined attitude and have tried to emulate it. As 2 Timothy 1:7 says, "For the Spirit God gave us does not make us timid, but gives us power, love and self-discipline." Luca's fighting spirit epitomized this verse.

We saw these traits on full display when Luca was four and a half years old and received his second diagnosis of brain cancer. I remember that sick feeling I had in the pit of my stomach as we returned to Rady Children's Hospital for Luca to begin the second autologous stem cell transplant (life-threatening, high-powered chemotherapy followed by a rescue of his own stem cells). He had endured his first treatment just one month before, which involved spending a month in the hospital hooked up to an IV.

He had no immune system, and the pain from sores down his esophagus required morphine and left him unable to eat. He had to be bathed every two hours during the day so the thiotepa (chemo) wouldn't leave him with permanent stains on his skin. Frank and I struggled to watch our son back in the same place where he had suffered so much trauma, where his body had been zapped of white blood cells, and where the treatment had left lasting damage on his entire being. There was also a good chance, we were told, that he would not be able to have children.

I had heard that at many children's hospitals around the country, returning children will often throw up or suddenly become nauseated because they subconsciously make the connection to their past pain. Did our sweet Luca remember the doctors, nurses, patient rooms, or smells? Was he confused about why he had to endure so much pain once more?

As caring and brilliant as the doctors and nurses at Rady are, and as special as the place is because of all the lives it has saved, there is still an underlying dimension of any children's hospital that makes every parent uneasy. You walk on fragile ground, surrounded by the bleak reality of death, loss, and grief. Everywhere you look, there are children and families enduring unfathomable circumstances. As I contemplated his return to the oncology wing, I wrote this honest prayer in my journal:

Dear Lord, I have decided that it is wise to put my prayers and contemplations on paper. The last two weeks have been so very shocking, difficult, and draining for our entire family. When Luca began his journey two years and three months ago, we prayed that you would heal him in Jesus's name and thought that you wanted us to do the treatment that was laid before us. Even after he was finished with his long, 18-month treatment, we prayed daily that Luca would remain healed and that one day in the future, he would be used for a wonderful testimony in your name.

Lord, when we received news that there was an area in his brain the size of a marble that needed to be biopsied and then ultimately, after the surgery when the medulloblastoma had returned, we were beside ourselves and felt as if we had been forgotten by you. Lord, I apologize for feeling that way now, but I still can't help but feel so many emotions, including anger, anxiety, and helplessness. Luca started his treatment at 10:00 p.m. today, and I feel very sad to have to see him endure more pain and suffering.

Has everyone forgotten that he is still just a little boy? He's only four, and this is the second time he's had to fight this horrible disease! I just want to take him in my arms and run away with him. I want to run away from everything that is not fun or encouraging or healthy. I want him to live a life filled with joy, not one filled with suffering. Please, Lord, I ask you with everything I have, allow this treatment to be as quick and painless as possible, and please, above all, allow it to be thorough in killing every last cancer cell in his little body. I want him in my life forever, and I can't handle the thought that we could lose him. I love him so much, Lord. Please heal my baby!

When your child gets diagnosed with cancer, it's not just him or her who gets diagnosed; your whole *family* gets diagnosed with cancer. We knew we were all on the brink of another brutal fight.

Amid all the anxiety of what had come before, the tragic need to return to the hospital, and the trauma that was again to come, we were shocked when Luca courageously *ran* into the hospital room, jumped onto the bed, and turned on his cartoons with excitement and purpose!

Our little warrior was ready for the doctors and nurses to do whatever they had to do next, ready to take on the world and kick cancer's butt once again.

His response floored us. We were learning from him that if he could get through it, we could get through it. Our Luca may have been innocent, but he was not ignorant. Children are often more in touch with their bodies than adults. We knew he felt weak. We knew he must have been confused, even though we carefully explained each procedure before it happened. We knew his body was experiencing a tremendous amount of pain as the treatments weakened him. By now, he knew where he was. He was not at Disneyland. Yet he *ran* to the hospital bed with determination and a mysterious sense of joy. His courageous spirit was contagious—a reminder to Frank and me that if our little boy could have an attitude like that, so could we.

I still find myself thinking of that scene today, in the years following Luca's death. He inspires me to *choose* to run into those rooms of my pain or unknowing and jump onto the fighting platform, ready to take it on headfirst. He inspires me to take the leap of faith.

Keep Going Through the Turmoil of the Valley

Something Christi always used to tell me was, "We just have to keep moving forward." She even had a semicolon tattooed on her arm to remind herself to keep going; to continue the sentence that was her life.

My sister suffered much in this life. But beneath that desire to escape her pain, she was also a fighter. Over the years, I saw her grow into someone who became unafraid to *engage* her pain. She was curious and empathic. She was a born-again Christian. She went to therapy frequently. She read many books about mental health and wanted to learn as much as she could. Her own struggles, in fact, are what propelled her to get her master's degree in psychology so she could help others navigate their own darkness—a darkness she knew well. She had survived up to that point and was determined to make the most of her life by helping others manage a darkness that is often difficult to understand. She fought relentlessly for a long time. Her suicidal thoughts might have overtaken her three times, but there were *hundreds* of times when she fought *through* them, when she kept living and loving, despite the dark veil that sometimes hung over her reality.

When we dare to fight whatever is trying to take us down, we position ourselves to be used by God for others—to be blessings, to be angels. Because Christi was willing to fight all those years, she was a blessing to me. Every day that we talked on the phone on her long drives to school, she made me feel less alone in my suffering. She helped give me the courage to keep fighting in the darkness of the valley. I have no idea where I'd be today without having had her love and counsel for all those years. It still hurts to know she chose to leave, and it still occasionally makes me angry. There was still so much more love and counsel we could have given to one another. I simultaneously cherish what she taught me while grieving the reality that so many more lessons in the vibrant heart and brilliant mind of hers will go unheard.

Her counsel was especially impactful to me when Gabriel, our third child, was ten months old. For some reason, at that time, everything Luca had previously been through caught up to me. Trauma *always* catches up to you. Grief *always* catches up to you. It had been an excruciating early journey through parenthood: two bouts of Luca's rare, serious form of brain cancer, our obsession with finding a cure and all the disappointments in between, and the brutal encounters with the crippling sting of death along the way. All the while, we were trying to give Grace and Gabriel the love and attention they deserved while running a marathon every day to provide the basic care Luca needed to stay alive.

Luca's survival of his second bout with brain cancer was called a medical miracle; the odds were essentially zero, we were told. After that fight, we settled into a "new normal."

My days were chaotic as a mother of three, one of whom had special needs and needed to be hand-fed fluids and food throughout the day. Luca's second diagnosis had been a serious blow, as he was just starting to eat on his own before the medulloblastoma returned. His two surgeries resulted in significant brain damage, and Luca needed a feeding tube for the next twelve years. Weighed down by so much grief and anxiety from the past and fear of the future, my sleeping problems became debilitating. *Really* debilitating.

I went three months without sleeping more than an hour or two a night. My heart rate skyrocketed. My body began to shake throughout the day. My stomach ached, and I had no appetite. It was a spiral from there. I lost a lot of weight. I wasn't exercising because I had no energy. I so desperately wanted to sleep, the most basic of human needs, but I couldn't even do that. Honestly, I thought I was dying.

As Gabor Maté wrote in a beautiful book my sister gave to me, *When the Body Says No*, "Emotions interpret the world for us. They have a signal function, telling us about our internal states as they are affected by input from the outside. Emotions are responses to present stimuli as filtered through the memory of past experience, and they anticipate the future based on our perception of the past."[1]

It was around this time that I was diagnosed with generalized anxiety disorder. For a long time after Luca's first diagnosis, we had been in life-or-death mode. Every MRI…every surgery…everything we were dealing with on a daily basis wore on us past the point of exhaustion. Luca was a wonderful child, but he was dependent on us for everything. We're human. Our bodies simply cannot continue operating normally while carrying around that much stress and trauma that we have not confronted or processed because of life's demands.

My conversations with Christi helped me carry on. She was willing to enter that dark place with me, and, rather than try to fix me, simply sit with me in the confusion. Sometimes her listening ear was just enough to fight through another day. Trauma, in a sense, has made me who I am, but the battle for me has been to not let it define me. It has affected my life, radically changing the ground I stand on, but it's been up to me to, like Luca, learn how to live with it and love myself and others the way God loves us.

Christi lives on through me today. My sister was a licensed counselor, and on the third anniversary of her death, I was able to counsel my first patient at CAPS (College Area Pregnancy Services) in San Diego as a trained patient-care specialist. I was able to show the young woman grace and acceptance—no judgment—just as Christi always showed me. I was able to give her all the information she needed to make an informed decision, just as Christi always did for me in helping me understand the landscape of my anxiety. And I was able to tell the young woman how much God loved her, just as Christi always taught me through her careful and empathetic posture of listening.

Yes, grief, with its darkness and heaviness, was overwhelming (and still is some days), but it also deepened my ability to love, empathize,

1. Gabor Maté, MD, *When the Body Says No: Understanding the Stress-Disease Connection* (Hoboken, NJ: John Wiley & Sons, 2011) 205.

and serve so I can meet others where they are in their own darkness. God can use your deepest darkness as a means of solidarity to be a light for others in theirs.

Keep Going in Grief, and Let Go

Semicolons take on a more nuanced meaning in the grief process. Moving forward sometimes feels like moving backward. Other times, it feels like there is never resolution, as if the sentence will never end. It can sometimes have a similar trajectory to high-powered chemotherapy: things have to get a lot worse before they can get better. The white-blood-cell count has to go down to zero before the body can begin to build itself back up again and hopefully rid itself of the cancer. Healing, in this sense, is not always linear. It's not always pretty. Grief is the same way. Truly grieving can sometimes take you deeper into messiness and complexity. Sometimes, it involves hitting rock bottom, yet still refusing to lose hope; daring to believe that the sentence is never done until *God* says it is done.

By definition, *trauma* is "a deeply distressing or disturbing experience: a personal trauma like the death of a child." *Psychological trauma*, according to the Substance Abuse and Mental Health Services Administration, is the "damage to the mind that occurs as a result of a distressing event." Trauma is often the result of an overwhelming amount of stress that exceeds one's ability to cope or integrate the emotions involved with that experience. As many psychologists have noted, our personalities actually develop based on coping mechanisms, which sometimes includes surviving trauma.

My family and I experienced long-term trauma, meaning that ours went on for years, not just one day or one week. We found ourselves in life-and-death mode for a long time. As a result of that, I found myself naturally ignoring my feelings, just so I could do what had to be done, just so I could make it through the day. There was so much I had to accomplish, so much I didn't have time to deal with. Consequently, the pain remained untouched on a deep psychological level.

Anyone who has small children knows there are endless demands on your time and energy already, but when you're busy with medical concerns on top of that, you find yourself doing what it takes to just survive. There was always a child who needed to be tube-fed or nursed or a medical procedure that needed to be done, either in or out of the hospital. It wasn't until our third child, Gabriel, was about ten months old (I was thirty-three), five years after Luca's first diagnosis, that my mind and body fell apart.

I wasn't sleeping, perhaps because Gabriel had to be nursed three or four times a night. But we were also far enough out from Luca's second diagnosis that things were calming down a little, which caused the past unprocessed pain to rise up within me. It began with horrible pain in my stomach that never let up. It felt like I had stomach acid twenty-four hours a day, which led to more sleepless nights. I would lie in bed all night with my eyes closed, but unable to sleep. My heart would pound inside my chest, and my mind would race.

People would ask me what it was racing about. Sometimes, it was the weirdest things: a song that I couldn't get out of my head or a conversation I had with someone earlier that day. It was almost as if my brain was trying to cope the best it could, having endured what it had. I imagine I must have been experiencing a chemical reaction to all the events and trauma over the years. Every night, I would lie there, my mind racing, my heart pounding.

In your stomach, you actually have a pulse. Have you ever felt your own? What's crazy is that I could actually *see* my stomach pulsating when I looked down at it from my pillow. My only reprieve was dozing off for two hours or so, but the moment I woke up, I would experience unrelenting anxiety. This went on for three months. I felt like I was staring down a giant, unable to see past my physical and emotional pain. Again, it truly felt like I was dying.

I have looked back at pictures of myself from that time, and it makes me really sad. I appear sickly. I could take a shower, fix my hair, and put makeup on so the average person couldn't see that something was wrong, but the truth is, I didn't know how much longer I could go on. I was dealing with emotions that, in turn, were creating biological havoc. All this was finally coming out half a decade after Luca's first diagnosis.

When you go long periods of time without sleeping, which is a basic need, you start to develop all kinds of other health problems. Sleep is one of the three pillars of health—the other two being nutrition and exercise. If one of those things is amiss, it will affect the other two things and, in turn, impact your entire life.

Each individual processes his or her feelings differently. Perhaps this has become a cliché, but it is true that time heals. Especially when you are trying to engage whatever challenge you're facing . I can now confidently tell you that no matter how bad it gets, it *will* get better. I promise. There will be improvement. There will be glimpses of resolve. But when you're absorbed in the "dark night of the soul," it's sometimes difficult to see the light.

But you do not have to figure it out right now. That's one of the underlying notions of anxiety— the idea that you have to figure it out *now*. But really, it's about taking it a day at a time and sometimes a minute at a time. Rest in the promises God has given. Try to feel His peace in the pain, even if it feels impossible.

One of the things that helped me, by the way, is medication. There is still a negative stigma about therapy and medication, especially in religious communities, but these routes should not be shamed. It's courageous to admit that you need help and then go out and find it. I'll admit that there was a time when I was against all pharmaceutical drugs because I have an education in natural medicine and could see the terrible effects that pharmaceuticals had on Luca. It's important to do your research, be cautious, be inquisitive with your doctor, and trust your own mind and body. What you might find is that some medication is incredibly helpful, even if it's temporary.

I felt ashamed when I began taking medication for depression, and I was careful not to tell anyone about it. As time went on, I became unapologetic about my own cross that I had to carry and the different things that helped me carry that cross. Medication for my depression and anxiety helped me be there for my children and the rest of my family. Medication helped by balancing the chemicals in my brain so I could sleep properly, get up each morning, press forward, and confront my pain.

We live in a fallen world. Even if we believe in God and His promises, we still have to deal with the sicknesses, depravities, and unfathomable injustices that confront us. Modern medicine is now almost universally accepted to treat physical ailments. We must move beyond the outdated stigma of using medicine to treat psychological ailments.

There are fewer nutrients in our food than there were fifty years ago, so even a healthy diet is not what our ancestors consumed. I think that's another reason why people struggle with their mental health sometimes—they're just not getting the nutrients they need. And people often don't sleep well because of the overstimulation they experience on their digital devices, often right before bed or in the middle of the night, when they wake up. And exercise becomes more difficult when we no longer hunt like our ancestors and instead sit on office chairs in cubicles forty hours a week. So much unhealthiness can be traced back to basic health pillars. And then there's trauma, on top of everything else, and the unique personality traits each of us has to navigate.

In my own battles with depression, anxiety, and sleeplessness, one of the most difficult things to change was my own inner dialogue. One of the first rules of self-care, I learned, is to refrain from beating yourself up. I sometimes beat myself up during my restless nights because I was unable to sleep, the most natural of human activities, which only made things worse. I just wanted to be "normal." It was easy to judge myself and cling to the question, "What's wrong with me?"

Thanks, in part, to an anxiety support group that Christi inspired me to attend regularly, I slowly began learning how to reframe my inner dialogue. Yes, sleeplessness was frustrating, but beating myself up only made it worse. It sent me into a spiral of anxiety, which only made it harder to sleep. So I began talking to myself with more compassion and understanding. *That* was where I was to wage my fight—in my own inner dialogue—not in whether or not I could sleep on a particular night.

I began saying things to myself the way I imagined God, in His radical love, would talk to me. Something like this: "My precious daughter, Elena, you have been through so much in parenthood. It's no wonder you are struggling to sleep. *Anyone* would struggle to sleep after all you've been through. Just know that I love you and that I'm with you. It might feel like I've abandoned you, but I have not. I'm so proud of you. I'll never leave you or forsake you."

Slowly but surely, cultivating more grace, curiosity, and compassion for myself in my thinking and in my prayers helped me relax, breathe, and sometimes even fall back asleep. Sometimes it didn't, but my thinking was healthier. Of course, seeking professional guidance and finding solutions in diet, natural medicine, and prescription medication helped as well. There is no shame in therapy. There is no shame in medication. As the popular saying goes, "It's okay to not be okay."

My insomnia still returns. Generalized anxiety disorder does not just go away. But when it does return, just as Luca's cancer returned, I'm learning to run into the room of my pain with a determined spirit and joyful heart. Luca had such a profound testimony because of how he fought the battles he faced. Maybe my depression, anxiety, and insomnia were *opportunities* for me to live out my testimony—to learn more about myself, to grow in my relationship with God, and to ultimately help others because of my willingness to fight, just as Luca inspired us through his courageous spirit.

Pain was not the end for him. It was the semicolon in a sentence that ultimately led to his testimony, his spiritual mission. Those battles look different for each of us. But no human being is exempt to suffering. *How* we suffer is up to us. God's love inspires us to extend compassion and grace to ourselves in the fight because God has infinite compassion and grace for us. Children are often a profound reflection of this love. Children with special needs have superpowers that we can learn from in our complex world of comparisons, demands, and perceptions. They can free us from the stuck places where our brains tend to cling to unknowing or negativity rather than gratitude or positivity; they can open the doors when we get trapped inside our heads and judge ourselves too harshly.

Luca never compared himself to others or judged himself by what he couldn't do. He never beat himself up. I know this is true because of how vibrant and joyful he always was. Of course he had his off days and blow-up moments, but those were few. Anyone who knew him will tell you that joy was the animating force of his life. He didn't get down on himself because he wasn't like everyone else. He simply lived the life that chose him. He fought the battles that found him. To him, life was really quite simple. His natural purpose was to love others and to be loved in return.

As Joshua 1:9 says, "Be strong and courageous. Do not be frightened, and do not be dismayed, for the LORD your God is with you wherever you go." Deuteronomy 31:6 echoes this notion: "Be strong and courageous. Do not fear or be in dread of them, for it is the LORD your God who goes with you. He will not leave you or forsake you."

Spiritual courage is not necessarily being visibly strong in a worldly sense, the way we might envision a superhero or star athlete. More often, strength and courage look a lot more subtle and quiet, like when our four-and-a-half-year-old son with special needs ran into that hospital room with so much determination and joy in his spirit. Spiritual courage is the willingness to run into the rooms of our pain, knowing that God is with us and that He loves us. Spiritual courage is the willingness to do the hard inner work and diagnose the lies you might be telling yourself—lies that contradict your identity in Christ—and let what God says about you become your truest reality. Spiritual courage is the willingness to, like Luca, suffer with grace rather than resorting to victimization or self-pity. Spiritual courage is the willingness to keep going, to use a semicolon instead of a period.

The fact that you are breathing and reading this is your cue that God still has work to do in you and through you, no matter what you're going through or what you've been through. Yet many have chosen a period over a semicolon by adopting the type of mindset that caves to fear. When we dare to keep going, we partner with God in allowing our testimony and ministry to evolve and continue.

During Luca's three bouts with cancer, the amazing medical team at Rady Children's Hospital modeled this kind of determination and contagious desire to never give up. Though Luca's situation sometimes looked bleak, they were determined to do everything they could. They kept seeking innovative ways to combat his cancer, and they accepted and integrated my husband's resourcefulness in searching out new treatment options. They were unafraid to accept that maybe they didn't have all the answers. They were humble enough to accept outside wisdom on numerous occasions—the expertise of other professionals who were on the front lines of pediatric research. They waged war against Luca's cancer again and again, and, even though the odds were stacked against them, they refused to throw up the white flag.

And they didn't just fight Luca's cancer with science; they fought it with the power of love. In an industry where health professionals are sometimes hesitant to develop personal connections with their patients, the doctors and nurses at Rady's became some of our closest confidantes. They cried with us. They prayed with us. Their hearts ached as our hearts ached. The first three people who spoke at Luca's memorial service were all from Rady's. They felt like Luca was something of an angel who had been sent to help them as well.

Dr. John Crawford, the director of neuro-oncology at Rady's, later told us that the second he looked into Luca's blue eyes, he thought, *I'm going to be in trouble with this one.* Luca had a way of tugging at the heartstrings of everyone he met. He didn't have to say a word to command the attention of those around him. Loved ones, close friends, and even acquaintances quickly developed deep compassion and respect for him after learning of his plight.

I love Hebrews 12:1–3: "Therefore, since we are surrounded by such a great cloud of witnesses, let us throw off everything that hinders and the sin that so easily entangles. And let us run with perseverance the race marked out for us, fixing our eyes on Jesus, the pioneer and perfecter of faith. For the joy set before him he endured the cross, scorning its shame, and sat down at the right hand of the throne of God. Consider him who endured such opposition from sinners, so that you will not grow weary and lose heart."

What would it look like for you to not grow weary, to refuse to lose heart? What would it look like for you to run into the room of your pain? To use a semicolon instead of a period and be courageous so God can use you to be a blessing to others?

Each of us has something in life that feels too heavy, too dark, or too overwhelming, but the sentence must not stop there. It must go on. God is the author, and it's up to us to enter fully His story.

CHAPTER 2

An Angel's Perseverance

After Luca's first brain surgery at age two, he was transferred to the ICU for recovery. Though we were thrilled to see him on the other side of such a serious surgery, we were also horrified by his condition. Having just had a craniotomy in which his skull was basically cracked open, he had a five-inch-long scar on the back of his head that continued down the back of his neck. His face was swollen and bruised. His right pupil was fixed in the corner of his eye and wouldn't move. His little face and body looked like he had been in a car accident. It broke our hearts to see our baby in this condition.

When my mom and stepdad came to visit, Luca was in the orthopedic unit. He had been in the ICU for four days and was in very bad shape, unable to play. They had brought Luca an orange stretchy toy as a recovery gift. My stepdad tied the toy to a traction band above Luca's bed, where patients' broken legs are sometimes elevated. Luca, almost immediately, locked his eyes on the toy, and every time my stepfather moved it, he laughed hysterically. He had to have been in excruciating physical pain. He had to have been frightened by the unfamiliarity of his experience. He had to have been confused. Yet he just kept looking up at the toy and laughing uncontrollably whenever his Poppy played with it.

Luca was naturally ministering to us—leading us through the wilderness of unknowing—without even knowing it. His ability to find joy in the most unlikely circumstances revealed a certain resiliency and perseverance that would animate him throughout his life as he confronted all the challenges he faced. Luca had a long journey ahead of him, and he had to have been absolutely miserable in his physical condition, but he somehow found joy in the most impossible circumstances—a profound example to all of us. Joy, as we would find out, fueled his perseverance. I think his joy came from the fact that he knew he was not alone. He was surrounded by people whom he loved and who loved him back.

Luca had everyday challenges for sixteen years that he had to overcome, yet he persevered. He couldn't eat or drink on his own or speak more than a few words. Things that most people take for granted, he couldn't do. But his life was not without joy. In fact, his life *was* joy, and it helped him and everyone around him to persevere. Luca was resilient and persevered in how he fought. We were resilient and persevered in how we fought *for* him. We have become well acquainted with perseverance.

In Exodus 14, we read about God guiding Moses and the Israelites out of Egypt as Pharaoh and his army chased after them: "Then the *angel* of God (emphasis mine), who had been traveling in front of Israel's army, withdrew and went behind them. The pillar of cloud also moved from in front and stood behind them, coming between the armies of Egypt and Israel. Throughout the night the cloud brought darkness to the one side and light to the other side; so neither went near the other all night long" (Ex. 14:19–20).

The chaos the Israelites faced as they fled Egypt, with the Egyptians in hot pursuit, under the guidance of this mysterious angel set a trajectory for their journey. Their post-slavery journey would be grueling, but God would remain beside them. Their path would wind deeper into the unknown, but they were not alone. Their journey would have dead-ends and desert phases, figuratively and literally, but there would always be a joy and hope accessible to them because of the wonders they witnessed.

In the book of Nehemiah, the minor prophet, Nehemiah, eight centuries after the Israelites' exodus, prayerfully reflects with gratitude on what God did for the Israelites during that time: "You saw the suffering of our ancestors in Egypt; you heard their cry at the Red Sea. You sent signs and wonders against Pharaoh, against all his officials and all the people of his land, for you knew how arrogantly the Egyptians treated them. You made a name for yourself, which remains to this day. You divided the sea before them, so that they passed through it on dry ground, but you hurled their pursuers into the depths, like a stone into mighty waters. By day you led them with a pillar of cloud, and by night with a pillar of fire to give them light on the way they were to take" (Neh. 9:9–12).

Some pastors and teachers criticize the Israelites for their lack of faith in the desert amid all the miracles that had been performed for them, but if your family had been enslaved for four generations, or if you had to wander through nothingness for forty years, you would probably get frustrated and discouraged, too. Nehemiah's words remind us of the Jewish people's bedrock tradition—their dedication to remember and savor what God had done for them, even as they faced persecution in the present. Perseverance has a longevity to it. The Israelites' journey to the Promised Land, overall, was marked by perseverance.

In their brutal, mysterious, confusing, wondrous journey we are reminded that we worship a God who pursues and perseveres. The Bible, from the Old Testament to the New Testament, tells the story of God's ever-expanding love. Despite our sins and screwups, our wandering and wickedness, God kept sending signs, miracles, prophets, angels, and, eventually, a savior. God's relentless pursuit of humanity from the beginning of time helps us to trust in His love today and, like Luca, root ourselves in joy because of the divine grace that surround us. God's love helps us to persevere in chaos and confusion. God is with us every step of the way, even when we have no idea where they were going.

You Are Not Alone

Before we knew what it was like to feel helpless, before Luca threw up spontaneously in the middle of his dinner, before the heartbreak of signing up for life-threatening surgery, our little Luca was a happy baby. When we learned that our two-year-old had medulloblastoma and was in a battle for his life, our battle began as well. I remember going into our meeting with Luca's oncologist at Rady Children's Hospital feeling downcast, to say the least. His diagnosis had blindsided us, and now we were desperate to know what the next steps were.

"First of all, I'm sorry to be with you under these circumstances," the oncologist said to us. "This is the toughest part of my job, and I can only imagine what the last few weeks have been like for you and your family."

Frank turned toward me and wrapped his arm around me. I think he could see I was on the verge of tears.

"Thank you for saying that, Doctor," he managed, "but how are we going to fight this?"

She cleared her throat. "I've looked over our treatment options, and the one I'm recommending is called the Children's Oncology Group Study P9934. It's a Phase 3 clinical trial, and I think Luca would be a good candidate."

A clinical trial? Part of a study? You mean that Luca's so bad off that he can't receive radiation or chemotherapy treatment like everyone else?

The oncologist must have seen the shock on our faces because she immediately set out to explain herself.

"I know what you're thinking, but the type of radiation that's normally done on pediatric patients is for children who are three, four, or five years old. They already know how to talk and do a lot of things. Because Luca just turned two, standard radiation treatment would do considerable damage to his brain."

"So, what can we do?" Frank asked. "If Luca is too young for radiation, is chemotherapy a better option?"

The doctor's face tightened. "If we just did the chemo without the radiation, then his chance for survival would be very low, so we want to bring these two types of treatments together. That's why I'm suggesting this clinical trial at the UC San Diego Medical Center. Luca would receive what we call 'conformal radiation,' which targets cancer cells in the tumor bed and minimizes damage to other areas of the brain. When the radiation treatment is over, we can follow up with chemotherapy. But I have to inform you that there are extreme risks involved with conformal radiation."

"What kinds of risks?" I asked.

"Severe. He might not survive the treatment, or he could become a vegetable. But if you choose not to be part of this clinical trial, there will be little we can do for him."

We sought a second opinion at St Jude Children's Research Hospital and were told the same thing—that the clinical trial would be Luca's best chance. The doctor told us that on a regular protocol for children a few years older than Luca they had historically seen five-year survival rates between 50 and 70 percent...but *that* was only if the child did the full radiation and full chemo, which Luca was unable to do because of his age.

That didn't exactly sound promising, but the clinical trial was Luca's best chance at survival. We were told, however, that it might cause damage to his normal brain tissue, impair his cognitive ability, or impair future fertility…and there was a risk of cancer coming back.

"How big is the risk of a secondary cancer?" Frank asked.

"We believe there's a 5 percent chance or less that he'll have a secondary cancer," the oncologist said, "but that number could be higher since he's only two years old."

I was having an extremely tough time dealing with the emotional somersaults of the preceding twenty-four hours. Everything had happened so quickly—first, the news that our son had a tumorous mass in his brain. But then, being informed that he'd have to undergo an immediate operation to remove the brain tumor was devastating. There was no time to even think about ramifications.

It had fast become a dire situation. One of the doctors explained that Luca's vomiting spells were a manifestation of the pressure on his brain from the tumor. And the mass was big—similar to the size of a small orange. I had a hard time imagining how any type of orange could fit into a cantaloupe, which was about the size of my baby's precious head at just two years old.

In this informational whirlwind, I felt more at peace when I was with Luca. The night before his surgery, I remember reading books together and tickling him as he was sitting up in his hospital bed. I wanted to be as upbeat as I could for him; I didn't want him to sense any of my fear. While Frank was gathering belongings at home, I fed Luca a bowl of Cheerios and milk. I knew this would be the last meal he could eat before surgery in the morning. My heart ached for our sweet boy. All I wanted to do was protect him from what was about to happen, but I was helpless to do so.

I also felt more at peace whenever I talked to Frank. He had experienced something miraculous the day before, when he told me that he had knelt next to the family room couch and prayed, "God, please come into our lives now. I really need You now, more than I've ever needed You, please. We can't do this without—"

Suddenly, at the end of his fervent prayer, he was interrupted by the sound of something crashing to the floor in the kitchen. He said he got goosebumps and felt an overwhelming sense of warmth all over his body. He had never felt anything like that before. He rose to his feet to investigate what happened and saw that a refrigerator magnet holding up a family photo and a laminated notecard had fallen to the kitchen floor. The notecard was an illustration of St. Francis de Sales, a seventeenth-century French prelate. Here is what it said:

> "Do not look forward to what might happen tomorrow; the same Father who cares for you today will take care of you tomorrow and every day. Either He will shield you from suffering or He will give you unfailing strength. Be at peace, then put aside anxious thoughts and idle imaginations."
> —St. Francis

At the bottom of the card was a Bible verse:

> "Be of good courage, and he shall strengthen thine heart."
> —Psalm 27:14 (KJV)

God's Word was a reminder that He would be with us every step of the way with Luca. We were not alone. Though it felt like we were drowning, God had not abandoned us. Like the Israelites—as they journeyed out of slavery, into the wilderness, toward the Promised Land—we had to trust that God would guide us every step of the way, even if a grueling journey awaited us.

On the back side of the laminated card were these words:

Life goes on from day to day.
God is always near.
There is a place for hope;
there is no place for fear.

Take heart and meet each minute
with faith in God's great love.
Aware that every day of life is
controlled by God above.

Never dread tomorrow

or what the future brings.
Just pray for strength and courage,
and trust God in all things.

Lift up your heart, have faith in God,
and say a fervent prayer,
For as you trust in Him, so He
will always keep you in His care.

When Jesus came to this world, He was less interested in explaining why there was so much suffering in this world and instead *entered* suffering. He was born in a humble manger and suffered an excruciating, humiliating death on a Roman cross. His very name, "Jesus," means "Emmanuel," which means "God with us." Jesus, among many other things, demonstrated to the human race that we are not alone.

I don't know why horrible things happen in this life. I don't know why suffering exists. I don't know why good people endure incomprehensible things. Through study, I have come to accept intellectually that we live in a fallen world and that with the gift of free will comes the curse of evil, imperfection, and loss. However, accepting it intellectually isn't the same as feeling a peace or acceptance about it in my heart. All I can say is that, through it all, just knowing that God was with us was enough to fuel our resiliency. It takes courage to keep going, but I would say it takes joy to persevere. There is a longevity to perseverance.

A life of perseverance is marked by choosing to be resilient, day after day after day. Luca epitomized this. He fought life-threatening brain cancer three times in merely sixteen years. Joy is different than happiness, and I've learned that joy—unlike happiness—isn't dependent on external circumstances. Joy is an attitude; joy perseveres and endures, regardless of the things that happen to us. When we realize that God is with us every step of the way, protecting us in His own mysterious way, it makes the burden a little lighter to carry. It allows us to, like the Israelites, take one step after another, amid the confusion, uncertainty, and doubt and to persevere in our joy anyway.

Even though our lives sometimes felt like they were falling apart, God never left us. He was ever-present, weeping as we wept. He held me up so I could overcome my world's circumstances, just as He has overcome the world. As Romans 8:18 says, "I consider that our present sufferings are not worth comparing with the glory that will be revealed in us." I also really like Romans 8:37–39, which reads, "No, in all these things we are more than conquerors through him who loved us. For I am convinced that neither death nor life, neither angels nor demons, neither the present nor the future, nor any powers, neither height nor depth, nor anything else in all creation, will be able to separate us from the love of God that is in Christ Jesus our Lord."

God had the power to teleport every single Israelite to the Promised Land, or even turn a nearby piece of land in Egypt into the Promised Land. But God didn't do that. Instead of acting like a genie for the Israelites, God showed His grace all the more by coming *alongside* them as they walked. God got dirty. He was not there to grant their wishes; he was there to enter the messiness of their lives. As they crossed the Red Sea. As they journeyed through the wilderness. As they wrestled and struggled and questioned along the way.

God's ways are not linear. No, far from it. But I believe He mysteriously comforts us in the intense heat of our trials with the coolness of a cloud and mysteriously guides us through the dark night of the soul with a pillar of fire. The simple fact that He is with us along the way helps awaken something of inner joy within. This mysterious joy sustains us, like the manna and quail God provided for the Israelites on their journey, like the cloud and pillar of fire that guided them. Joy is always accessible, even if the journey is brutal, because we begin to encounter God in a way we've never experienced before.

After Luca's surgery, one of the surgeons let us know that he had to do a little scraping on the left side of Luca's brain to try to remove all of the tumor. It didn't matter that he was one of the best pediatric surgeons in the world—that's just how complicated the surgery was. This little scrape ended up paralyzing Luca on the right side of his body.

We were already reeling from the life-or-death scenario we found ourselves in. This news caught us off guard and was just as gut-wrenching. How could this be happening? Our innocent child was now unable to play like he had before…or walk…or eat by himself. We didn't know it at the time, but it would be ten months before he would walk again.

Even though it felt like our lives were falling apart, we knew God was with us and encouraging us each day. You might be wondering, *How?*

Because of the light in our son.

Some way, somehow, Luca always seemed happy and content. He didn't complain. He rarely cried. It was almost as if he knew this was the journey he was supposed to be on. His smile and his laughter encouraged us every day. It was how God spoke to us. His joy was the cloud and pillar of fire God used to let us know that we were not alone.

In your own seasons of struggle and darkness, you may find that God will use people around you to guide the way.

When we celebrated Luca's second birthday in the hospital, I took him to the playroom, and his face lit up as I read *Dragons Love Tacos* to him. When the physical and occupational therapists would come to his room to help him do his daily exercises, he would laugh when he couldn't move his arm or his leg the way he could before. His humor was certainly contagious, and even though we were pushing through our own anger and confusion over what was happening, we found ourselves laughing with him. We probably looked into the eyes of Luca the way the Israelites might have stared up at those towering walls of the parted Red Sea—perhaps exhausted by life but simultaneously overcome with spiritual wonder and hope. For God was with us and was not about to leave us.

Keep Your Eyes on the Promised Land

Sometimes in life, you're dropped in the middle of the wilderness. And sometimes this wilderness stretches out in all directions, leaving you wandering for years. Trauma and grief are like that. You might find yourself disoriented and wondering, *How did I get here? Why is this the path I'm on? Where is God in all this confusion and suffering?* All you can do is focus on the next step and cling to hope, even when it feels unreachable.

Just as the Israelites focused on the Promised Land as they journeyed through the wilderness, we remained focused on the ultimate prize for Luca for sixteen years: his health, well-being, and, ultimately, finding the cure for our son.

We were relieved and thankful when Luca went into remission for nearly two years.

After he turned four, we took him in for his regular MRI. Normally, we didn't hear MRI results for a day or two, and we had learned that no news was good news when it came to these sorts of things. The brain damage he had suffered from his first surgery and radiation treatment was becoming clearer as he grew and developed, but we were grateful for his remission. We knew he would face many challenges in life because of his special needs, but we hoped cancer would never again be a battle he'd have to face.

That evening, we received a phone call. The caller ID said "Children's Hospital." Frank picked up the phone. It was our oncologist. Frank could hear her urgency.

"Frank," she said, "I got the preliminary MRI results from the radiologist, and then I took a look myself. From what we can see, it looks like there's a new lesion on the frontal lobe. It's only a centimeter and a half long, but there's no question something new is there."

We knew what she was saying.

Luca had cancer...again.

It was later confirmed that the medulloblastoma had returned.

Before we knew it, we were sending Luca into the operating room once more, hoping his neurosurgeons would be able to remove the lesion. But as doctors ran tests post-surgery and conducted MRIs, we learned that more cancer cells were inhabiting Luca's brain, despite the doctors' surgical heroics. Microscopic and malignant cells were continuing to divide and multiply, which was obviously horrible news.

We were told that we were running out of medical options. About the only thing we hadn't tried was something called an Ommaya reservoir, a plastic device that would be implanted under Luca's scalp and be used to deliver a different type of chemotherapy. Our oncologist explained that the reservoir would allow technicians to put a new type of chemo down Luca's spine. It would then travel into his brain via the spinal fluid.

The problem was there were many side effects. The Ommaya reservoir was well known for causing nausea, vomiting, headaches, and a stiff neck. We were told that most patients did not tolerate the device well. This was the other problem: the doctors told us that the procedure *would not* save Luca's life—it would only buy him time. But it seemed like our last grasp.

We were communicating with two oncologists at the time, and neither would say Luca was terminal. But they definitely left the impression that there wasn't much we could do for him beyond the Ommaya reservoir and that we should be prepared accordingly. The insertion of the reservoir would be the end of the line for treatment options. Otherwise, we were looking at palliative care—making Luca comfortable in the final months of his life.

While all this was happening, I was doing everything I could to care for Luca in the best way possible. He was receiving excellent nutrition via his feeding tube; going to physical, occupational, and speech therapy; and, of course, getting lots of love. And Frank was going to the ends of the Earth to find a cure, applying his focused mind to researching and networking at a superhuman level. We really made quite a team. My newfound calling in recent years as Luca's caregiver created the space for Frank to do what he does best: gather information. Day after day, often deep into the night, he sat at our computer and researched the newest cutting-edge scientific discoveries in pediatric brain cancer, sometimes contacting oncologists who were on the front lines.

Frank reached out to Memorial Sloan Kettering Cancer Center in the heart of New York City, reputed to be one of the top hospitals in the world for oncology, and explained our situation in an email to a nurse case manager. He did the same thing with MD Anderson in Houston, Cincinnati Children's Hospital, City of Hope in Los Angeles, and St. Jude's Children's Research Hospital in Memphis.

We were thrilled that a number of oncologists from these hospitals responded quickly and said they would look into Luca's medical records. We were discouraged, however, when two of the top oncologists in the United States told us we should begin to "think quality of life" for our son. We obviously appreciated the time they gave to Luca's case and their honesty as well, but their conclusions that we had "done everything we could" forced us to confront our deepest fears—that this was indeed the end—a period on our boy's precious life at only four years old.

But the conclusions these doctors shared only made Frank more determined. Like a mad scientist, he was determined to find *something* out there that could help Luca in this dire situation. Frank was finding that the survival rate of the reservoir procedure—the odds of living five more years—was a mere 5 percent, meaning that Luca's situation seemed hopeless.

Frank would later tell me that in confronting this hopelessness, one evening he prayed, *God, please give me a sign.*

A sign was forthcoming. He went back to his piles of research and looked at a new tree of website searches. He came across a link to a study of childhood medulloblastoma written by Dr. Jonathan Finlay, a pediatric neuro-oncologist specializing in the management of children, adolescents, and young adults with brain tumors. The article, printed in an oncology medical journal, contained a lot of dense medical terminology about "desmoplastic nodular medulloblastoma." The article seemed to describe the way pediatric patients with recurrent medulloblastoma responded when they were given high-dose, platinum-based chemotherapy followed up by a stem cell transplant, a technique also known as "stem cell rescue." In this particular clinical trial, the pediatric patients had a survival rate of 30 percent.

Frank shared the study with me, and that figure leaped out at me as well: *30 percent*. That may not seem very high—and it wasn't—but 30 percent was *six times* greater than the death sentence Luca had received. As we read deeper into the medical paper, however, we realized the sample group had only comprised fifteen children. That wasn't a large group, but we were grasping at straws.

What about Dr. Finlay's medical credentials? Did they measure up?

It turned out they were gold-plated. Dr. Finlay graduated from the University of Birmingham Medical School in England and had completed internships in general surgery at City General Hospital, Stoke-on-Trent. He'd done residencies in pediatrics at Birmingham Children's Hospital and in pediatric oncology at the Christie Hospital in Manchester. Described as a "thought leader" in his field, he had written or cowritten hundreds of medical studies that were published in peer-reviewed medical journals. From the glowing praise we found, he was a rock star in the world of pediatric oncology.

But how to reach him? It wasn't like we could Google his name and expect to find his personal cell phone number. But we needed to reach him *immediately*. The fact that this was urgent is an understatement. In just a few hours, Luca was to undergo an operation that we weren't sure was the best option.

We needed a miracle.

We prayed and asked God to help us find a phone number or an email address. Frank frantically but methodically searched for Dr. Finlay's name and found more medical studies and papers he had published. He painstakingly looked through each one. Then, at the bottom of one medical study Dr. Finlay had written, Frank saw an email address underneath his name. The study, though, was a decade old. Was that email address still active?

Frank decided to give it a shot anyway, as he always did. He wrote an impassioned message explaining our situation—that our doctors were telling us Luca had no chance and we needed to be thinking about palliative care. Was there any other type of treatment available? Was there something we had overlooked? He mentioned we were scheduled to have an Ommaya reservoir inserted into Luca's skull first thing in the morning.

"Can you please help us?" Frank wrote at the end of the email. "Can you please respond and give me some ideas on what we could do?" Frank remained focused on our goal: saving our son's life.

And then he sent the email into the ether, and we prayed for an answer that would come before the scheduled procedure, just a dozen hours away.

Twenty minutes later, incredibly, a miracle happened. We received a response—from Dr. Finlay! Here is what his message said:

> Dear Frank,
>
> I'm really sorry to hear about your son Luca. I'll certainly try to help you. Definitely cancel your surgery tomorrow. I know all the studies, and an Ommaya reservoir is not going to work or improve his chances of survival. My recommendation is that you use a platinum-type chemotherapy, followed by a stem cell transplant, because those procedures could significantly increase his chances of cure and survival rate. Send me your oncologist's phone number, and I will speak with her.
>
> Warmly,
> Dr. Jonathan Finlay

What's even crazier is that it was 6:00 in the evening on the West Coast, which meant it was 2:00 in the morning in Great Britain—the middle of the night. How had it happened that Dr. Finlay had seen the email and written back? It had to be a miracle. It's difficult to express how excited we were that a world-renowned oncologist, living in England, would respond to a desperate father in California at two o'clock in the morning, his time.

When Frank showed me the email, we were in total agreement: we had to postpone the Ommaya reservoir procedure until Dr. Finlay could talk to the pediatric oncologists at Rady's.

It turns out that Dr. Finlay's insight would save Luca's life. Dr. Finlay got intricately involved in the process, talking to our oncologists several more times and directing them in this cutting-edge procedure. He really took an interest in our son.

Luca's oncologists adopted the procedure Dr. Finlay recommended, and, through a painful and risky stem cell transplant, MRIs confirmed that Luca's tumor had somehow shrunk. We were ecstatic. Days before, we were told that we needed to think about "quality of life"—and now his cancerous tumor was *shrinking.*

His recovery was an up-and-down journey, though. Luca's red blood cells, white blood cells, and platelet counts had been knocked down to zero, meaning he had nothing with which to fight infection from germs or bacteria. Despite our best efforts to protect him, he somehow contracted a bacterium known as *Clostridium difficile* (also known as *C. diff*), which caused horrible, constant diarrhea and terrible redness on his bottom. He also experienced constant nausea. He cried when the diarrhea came on, and changing fifteen to twenty diapers a day was unpleasant for everyone. But as soon as we would clean him up, the smile would reappear on his face.

Luca was determined to get better.

Because of the success of the stem cell transplant, our oncologists wanted us to go home and return two weeks later for a second round. The medical consensus was: *Let's keep doing what Dr. Finlay says.*

Luca had such an incredible spirit that when we returned, he didn't appear to be upset or fearful. Again, he ran to his hospital room, jumped on his bed, and gave high fives to nurses who dropped in to say hello to him. He knew something bad was coming but was happy to be around people who loved him. My son amazed me.

After the second round, the MRI results came back even more positive and gave our doctors the confidence to tell us that Luca's cancer was gone!

The results from Dr. Finlay's groundbreaking study were not well known or widely accepted. But Frank had managed to find that *one* study, revealing *one* treatment option other than certain death, leading to *one* paper with an old email address, enabling Frank to send *one* email in the middle of the night, which led to connecting with *one* doctor, which led to him investing in *one* child. That unlikely chain of events ultimately rid Luca's body of a cancer that was trying to take his life, with only one night to spare.

Never forget that love is always worth the fight. You'll never regret giving your very all for those whom you love. As you journey out of captivity from whatever is holding you, into the wilderness, and as your days in the desert begin to run together, it might sometimes feel like you aren't going anywhere at all, like you're never going to get where you want to be. It might sometimes feel monotonous. It might sometimes feel hopeless. But don't take your eyes off the Promised Land. Keep looking up at the sheltering cloud during the day and the pillar of fire at night, trusting that you are being led somewhere. Notice the joy that surrounds you, even in life's complexity. Look into the eyes of those you love. Listen to the laughter of those you love. It will be the fuel to your perseverance.

It was very much a kind of desert-like feeling taking care of Luca during that decade and a half. Even after he was officially declared to be in remission, there was always a fear his cancer would return. We didn't know what the complications would be from his chemotherapy, radiation, and surgeries. There was so much mystery and uncertainty in the different clinical trials he was a part of. The energy all this required led to shifts in our relationships with family and friends. We became more difficult to relate to. At times, it was lonely. But we stayed focused and refused to lose sight of our ultimate goal.

The Israelites knew it would be a brutal journey through the wilderness, but what was most important for them was that they stayed focused on the Promised Land and trusted God along the way. It was important for them to find hope and joy in the fact that God was with them and was guiding them, even in their unknowing, even in their anxiety and fatigue. They had to keep believing that as long and grueling the journey might become, the Promised Land—the hope for a better tomorrow—was worth it. Love is *always* worth fighting for.

The fight might be tiring and all-consuming. It might feel like there is no escape. Think about the Israelites. Not a day went by—for forty years!—that they *weren't* journeying toward the Promised Land. Though they had some slip-ups along the way, overall, they kept their eyes on the prize. Some even died on their journey and never reached the Promised Land on this side of heaven, but as a people, they persevered. Their focus fueled their journey. And our focus fueled ours.

As God guided us, we never took our eyes off the Promised Land. We had days when we retired to bed hopeless, but by the next morning, I was ready to take care of our baby, and Frank was always ready to get back on the computer and search for a cure. He left no stone unturned.

The Wilderness of Grief

After Luca's first surgery to remove his tumor, he had twice-a-month chemotherapy treatments, performed at Rady's pediatric oncology clinic on Saturday mornings. These lasted more than a year. Most of the time, we'd have to stay at Rady's the entire weekend, and even into Monday, because Luca needed an immense amount of IV fluids to flush the chemo out of his system. Luca was only two years old. He had no idea what was going on. Though Luca would excitedly say, "Car, car, car!" any time we went to the hospital, it felt like we were driving him straight to hell.

For the protocol, doctors started him with Vincristine, a commonly used chemotherapeutic agent. The first time I saw the nurse who would be administering the drug, my anxiety level shot through the roof. She was dressed in a hazmat protection suit, complete with gloves, mask, and booties, and her hair was pinned back.

You're introducing this bag of poison into my son's body? And you can't even touch it?

One night, I broke down in front of Frank. "We can't do this anymore!" I cried out. Nothing in my being was okay with this. Every day, I could see signs of physical decline in my son. Even though I knew this was to be expected, I wasn't prepared for it. How could I ever be prepared for this?

The next day, I had to speak with the hazmat nurse. I told her how concerned I was and how upset I had been. I'm sure I was brushing away tears.

The oncology nurse struck an encouraging tone. "He's going to be okay," she said. "From what I've seen with the kids in this unit, they tolerate chemotherapy really well."

Frank did his best to lift my spirits. "We're gonna take it one day at a time," he said. "As soon as we get through this, then we'll have Luca back, and he will be healthy again. That's what we have to focus on.

That's all we can do."

One day at a time. That's what perseverance takes.

As the Israelites journeyed through the wilderness, at one point they grew frustrated and desperate that they did not have any water to drink. In Exodus 17, we read that they had seen God miraculously provide for them manna and quail—not to mention the guiding angel, the cloud, and the pillar of fire that accompanied them! Nonetheless, they began to doubt that God would take care of them when they grew thirsty. They petitioned to Moses in Exodus 17:3, "Why did you bring us up out of Egypt to make us and our children and livestock die of thirst?" Moses asked them why they quarreled with him and put the Lord to the test. Exodus 17:7 tells us that the Israelites continued to put the Lord to the test, saying, "Is the Lord among us or not?"

That question, "Is the Lord among us or not?" was at the very foundation of their grief and confusion as they journeyed through the wilderness. And understandably so, perhaps. They had been enslaved for hundreds of years. They would wander for decades. But they scapegoated Moses in their grief and pointed the finger at the very person who led them out of slavery. Their emotion was honest, raw, and real. Despite how frustrating the Israelites must have been to Moses, they remind us that we, too, can be sincere with God as we process the traumas of life.

Scapegoating in the wilderness is natural for humans. It's part of the denial and anger stages of grief. When Luca was diagnosed again at fifteen, I believed with all my heart and soul the Lord would heal him completely. When it became clear with each passing day that the Lord had planned something different, I wrestled. I wanted Luca to live a long, full life. I was convinced it would glorify God so much more if Luca were to survive because we would have such an amazing testimony to share with the world. I became angry. I pointed the finger at God. And again, this is natural, and human. We should not feel ashamed for scapegoating in our wrestling. God understands our hearts because He created us.

But we must not stay there. Persevering in the wilderness of grief requires us to engage each step of the grief process sincerely. Like Luca in his various life-and-death battles throughout his life, opening our eyes to the grace we've received and the divine joy that is always accessible to us can empower us to face our grief head-on.

In Katie Davis Majors' *New York Times* best-selling book *Daring to Hope*, a story about adopting and mothering thirteen girls and the tragedy that struck her family, she writes transparently about the grief process—her struggle to believe that God was good and that He really loves us amid life's incomprehensible pain. She writes these profound words:

> The world would teach us that pain is what ruins us. We are trained and conditioned to run from pain at all costs. Some would even argue that doing so is primal instinct. Only the supernatural working of the Holy Spirit can override this fear of pain with a love that is greater. The world would teach us that once we are broken, we cannot be used, we cannot be strong, we cannot be happy. But this is not true. In the very greatest miracle of all time, our Father God resurrects His Son Jesus out of the dark tomb and conquers death. After the brutal beating and scourging and mocking that is a direct result of the ugliness of my sin, Jesus whispers, 'Father, forgive them." And he does. Out of the black of the tomb, new Life emerges and new Light shines forth. The Lamb, the Lamb. God uses all things, even pain, for His glory.[1]

We didn't know it at the time, but as Luca approached his last days, Frank and I were already starting our journey through the classic "five stages of grief" pioneered by Swiss psychiatrist Elisabeth Kübler-Ross in the late 1960s: denial, anger, bargaining, depression, and acceptance. Those five stages were scary, and often overwhelming. It sometimes felt unending because we found ourselves moving back and forth through the stages rather than progressing straight through them in a tidy line.

Like the Israelites journeying through the wilderness, for some it might take a lifetime to fully grieve the trauma they've experienced. But never forget Katie Davis Majors' words: God can use all things, even pain, for our good and the good of others who are suffering. The cross reminds us that in our darkest night of the soul, we are not alone. God entered fully into the pain of the human experience through His Son.

---

1. Katie Davis Majors, *Daring to Hope: Finding God's Goodness in the Broken and the Beautiful* (New York: Penguin Random House LLC, 2017), 61.

The Gospel reminds us that Christianity does not offer a God who is removed from our reality but one who is intimately involved with our journey, even as we move through the confusion of the wilderness.

In some ways, it seemed like we never made it to the Promised Land because Luca's cancer did indeed return eleven years later. But at the same time, God gifted us with eleven more years with our precious son. Some of the top oncologists in the world had told us when he was four years old that we should start thinking about "quality of life" and palliative care. But God had other plans and worked wonders through Dr. Finlay. We were witnesses of the impossible coming to fruition. We didn't get the miracles we asked for—complete healing and a long, natural life for Luca—but his survival to a third battle with cancer after a pediatric diagnosis was a miracle in itself, with this written testimony to prove it.

Today, as I continue to grieve Luca's passing, I find myself thinking a lot about those eleven extra years that God gifted us with Luca's presence.

Just the other day, in fact, as I was cleaning the house, I saw something brown and crusty on the window covering in the office. I realized as I got closer it was old food from three years before, when the home nurse (whom we had brought in to help with Luca during the last months of his life) had tried to feed Luca. As she was feeding him, the tube kinked, and it squirted all over me, the nurse, Luca, and the window covering. Luca, always amused, started cracking up with his contagious squeal. The place was a mess. *We* were a mess. But Luca got us all laughing. We shared a moment. Each day is *filled* with moments like these! It was impossible not to laugh in the presence of someone who got so much joy out of such a challenging life. You'd better believe I didn't scrub that window covering when I noticed the remains of such a fond memory. There it sits today.

In grief, you have to do what works for you. Leave nasty brown crust on the blinds if you like, or clean them if it brings you peace. The grieving process is yours, and there's no right or wrong way to do it. Just keep venturing *through* the process; keep going. I have known bereaved parents to leave their child's room untouched for years. I've known others who cleared it out quickly because it was too painful to see. Moving forward through grief—perseverance—looks different for everyone.

We've given some things away—things that don't evoke good memories. But there is plenty that we hold onto. We still have Luca's THC and CBD in the refrigerator, for example, which his doctors recommended to help alleviate his pain. We were wary of giving it to him, but desperate times called for desperate measures. Medical marijuana isn't legal in every state and obviously is not appropriate for everyone, but whenever one of us opens the refrigerator and sees it still sitting there, we're reminded of the first time we administered it to Luca via his feeding tube. After about ten minutes, he began laughing hysterically and then, of course, the rest of us couldn't hold back. The kitchen was booming with our entire family laughing uncontrollably. I can almost hear that laughter when I open the fridge.

Just a few weeks ago, my daughter's boyfriend was over at our house for an afternoon swim. He forgot his swim trunks, and Grace said to me, "Gabriel's won't fit; maybe Luca's will." A year before, I might have told Grace not to get into Luca's things quite yet, but at this point, I was ready.

"Of course, see if they fit," I told Grace.

Next thing I knew, Grace's boyfriend was waltzing down the stairs, exuberantly modeling Luca's swim trunks and the baby-blue bucket hat that Luca always wore in the pool. I couldn't help but think about how hilarious Luca would have thought it was to see someone else model some of his favorite clothes. We were all cracking up. I could almost see and hear Luca laughing. I could almost taste his joy again.

Use the joyful moments God has gifted you to keep you moving through the wilderness. Be resilient—unafraid, curious, and determined to confront each challenge in the wilderness—as you grieve. You are not alone. Stay focused on honestly confronting the next challenge. The wilderness of grief might be where your healing begins and where the most important part of your journey will unfold.

My mom has mentioned to me on several occasions that we are now living for Luca and Christi because their lives were cut short. I love this notion. So, when we have fun experiences, we are doing it for them. Yes, we are living for Christ and for ourselves, but also for them. We are connected to them in Christ. Their lives fuel our perseverance. Their lives fuel our desire to journey well on our pilgrimage, and I believe that makes them happy in heaven.

CHAPTER 3

An Angel's Acceptance

One of the most inspiring characteristics of angels in the Bible is their acceptance of the assignments that God gives them. Not only do these assignments require them to leave heavenly perfection and enter fully the brokenness and pain that exists on Earth; these assignments are also not always glamorous. They often involve meeting people in the messy aspects of their lives—in the very valleys of their journeys.

One of the best examples of this might be the angel who wrestled Jacob throughout the duration of the night, a mysterious encounter that scholars and theologians have studied for centuries. Think about how crazy that would be! Jacob was no saint. He took his baggage and complicated past into that wrestling match.

In my mind, though, like all Scripture, the encounter tells us something loving and interesting about God. The angel's willingness to meet Jacob where he was and wrestle with him for hours is another revelation of God's intimate love for us. It is a reminder that God will meet us where we are in our confusion, transition, and pain. He loves us so much that He is willing to wrestle with us as we sincerely question and work out the complexities of our faith. Our past deception, baggage, and sin are never too much for Him. Our doubts, struggles, and questions are never too much for Him. He can handle it.

Of course, the Bible tells us that not all angels were willing to accept assignments. Lucifer, a fallen archangel, did not want to worship God because he wanted to be worshipped himself. As the Lord says in Ezekiel regarding the banishment of Lucifer, "Your heart became proud on account of your beauty, and you corrupted your wisdom because of your splendor. So I threw you to earth; I made a spectacle of you before kings" (Eze. 28:17). In being unwilling to accept the unique life and purpose God had given him, Lucifer not only caused suffering on this Earth but also caused suffering for himself: eternal separation from God.

Jesus, of course, is the best example of what it looks like to accept a divine assignment. Jesus, fully God and fully human, lets us know it's okay for us to struggle to *accept* our divine assignment, to wrestle with God as we *encounter* that assignment, and ultimately trust God as we partner with Him in fully *embracing* our divine assignment. Jesus gives us permission to be human.

We read about Jesus's anguish in the Garden of Gethsemane. He knows that is coming for Him when he cries out to God, "Won't you take this cup from me?" When he is crucified, He even cries out to his Father, "My God, my God, why have you forsaken me?" So emotionally raw and honest is His wrestling, it inspires us to be just as sincere as we engage our own journeys and pray honestly to God on those journeys.

Luca was the little soul who inspired us to accept our divine assignment with the same grace and joyful attitude that he accepted his. "Angel Boy" and "Love Man" were the best nicknames I could have given him. He was the brave little soul from John Alessi's book who willingly went into the world—*our* world—accepted his plight, suffered, and unlocked the goodness and love in our hearts.

Accepting an Unwelcome Change

I was ten years old when my dad's new business venture inspired a drastic cross-country move for our family: from Oklahoma to an apartment on Lemon Avenue in La Mesa. It was a bit of a cultural shock living in Southern California, and on top of that, my parents weren't getting along. Money was tight, and my mom wanted more stability. Eventually, she decided she wanted a divorce.

After the divorce was official, my dad saw Christi and me on weekends, but when he would come by the apartment to pick us up, there were arguments. His and my mom's relationship was strained, and it was only worsening. After a while, my father felt it was too complicated to be in the same city with us and moved out of state. His departure devastated me.

They say that being a single mother is the most difficult job there is. Mom, who was an interior designer at Ethan Allen, worked hard and did the best she could under trying circumstances. But it was still difficult and life altering to not have my dad near me.

After I completed seventh grade, my parents agreed that Christi and I would spend the summer with my dad in Great Barrington, Massachusetts, where he was managing a thousand-acre land development. Dad kept us with him beyond what was agreed on and sent us to school. Mom wasn't happy about that.

As warm summer afternoons turned to crisp autumn mornings, I remember seeing the leaves of the trees turn crimson red and bright orange—a change of seasons I'd never experienced in San Diego. It was so much fun to jump into a pile of raked-up leaves, and—after the first snowfall—to make snowballs and throw them at our new friends.

One afternoon, the last bell of the day rang at school, and I gathered my belongings as usual; but then, waiting outside my classroom was… *Mom!* Standing next to her was a man I'd never seen before. None of us knew she was coming.

"What are you doing here?" I asked. She was three thousand miles from La Mesa.

"We're here to pick you up and bring you home."

"Home?"

"Yeah. San Diego."

My universe turned upside down. Even though I loved my mom and missed her, I started to protest because I hadn't anticipated this. Nevertheless, I got in the car, and we drove to pick Christi up from her friend's house. I don't recall picking up my things, but that doesn't mean it didn't happen—childhood trauma has a way of making you forget details. I don't remember saying good-bye to my dad. It felt like we started the long drive back to San Diego almost immediately.

The man behind the wheel was Fred Smith (not his real name). In my opinion, this man took advantage of my mom's difficult financial situation and tried to make her dependent on him in her vulnerable state. I didn't know it at the time, but he turned out to be a very evil man.

At the age of thirteen, I was confused, baffled, and bewildered by this turn of events. When we reached Las Vegas, Fred turned off the Strip and parked next to a courthouse.

"What are we doing here?" I asked from the backseat.

"We're getting married," my future stepdad replied.

I became irate and insisted on staying in the car. Christi, nine at the time, was more malleable. She accompanied my mom and Fred into the courthouse, where a justice of the peace pronounced them husband and wife. I had just been uprooted and wasn't on board with their marriage. Can you imagine sitting in the car as your mom gets married to a man you have just met? I wasn't going to allow this man to be my dad, and my attitude toward him set the tone for a contentious household during my teen years.

Children don't plan to have parents who fight or a divided household, and no child envisions being ripped out of his or her school because of a custody battle and forced to live with a new father. Those were challenging years that required lots of adjusting and, I'm sure, planted deep seeds of instability and insecurity within me.

I could feel all that confusion rushing back into my reality when Luca was diagnosed with medulloblastoma one week before his second birthday. This quote from Maté's *When the Body Says No* has resonated with me since the very moment I read it:

> The way people grow up shapes their relationship with their own bodies and psyches. The emotional contexts of childhood interact with inborn temperament to give rise to personality traits. Much of what we call personality is not a fixed set of traits, only coping mechanisms a person acquired in childhood. There is an important distinction between an inherent characteristic, rooted in an individual without regard to his environment, and a response to the environment, a pattern of behaviours developed to ensure survival.[1]

When you decide to start a family with the person you love, you know there are going to be parenting challenges, but you certainly never envision spending days and nights in the oncology unit of a pedi-

1. Gabor Maté, MD, *When the Body Says No*, 127.

atric cancer hospital. You never envision your child not being able to formulate sentences or eat on his own. You never envision your child not having much of a social life as he grows older and being entirely dependent on his parents. No, you see your child growing up, having sleepovers with friends, causing trouble with friends, and getting their driver's licenses. You see yourself crying as they go off to college, crying again as they marry, and crying again when they have their first child.

Everything changed so quickly when Luca was first diagnosed. Before his surgery and treatments, he had been a toddler who was eating finger foods on his own, riding his tricycle, and walking and running around the house, as toddlers do. But once his chemotherapy started, he stopped eating. It made him so nauseated. He was unable to walk because of damage to his cerebellum (the area of the brain responsible for gross motor ability) he had suffered during surgery. We were all blindsided by a new normal.

By the time Luca's medulloblastoma returned two years later, when he was four, we were already beginning to see the long-term effects the first surgery and year-long treatment had on his brain. We were faced with another new normal: raising a child with special needs. As many parents raising a child like this will tell you, it would turn out to be one of the greatest divine gifts we've ever received, but it did not come without its challenges and adjustments.

The biggest adjustment was that I became Luca's full-time caregiver. It made the most sense for our family because Frank's job was stable. So, for the next twelve years, when Luca wasn't in his special day class at school, I spent almost every waking moment with him, helping him with his daily activities—bathing or dressing him; taking him to doctors' appointments; and ultimately adopting the role of physical therapist, speech therapist, and occupational therapist. Because he ate and drank very little on his own, I gave him fluids every few hours and fed him four times a day.

We began the day with 12 ounces of organic strawberry, peach, or blueberry liquid yogurt. For lunch, I'd prepare a smoothie, mixing up organic kale or spinach, banana, blueberries or raspberries, full-fat almond or oat milk, flaxseed oil, chia seeds, whole-grain cereal, raw almond butter, probiotics, and lots of love—all the good nutrients that were required to give him the best possible health. For a snack, liquid yogurt. And for dinner, different varieties of delicious home-made blended vegetable soups that my mother-in-law, (his Nonna) Lea, faithfully made for many years.

We had to be deliberate in getting calories and fat into him to keep Luca's weight up because he didn't eat enough on his own to thrive. Each day, especially when we were first thrust into this new way of living, involved lots of troubleshooting and experimentation because Luca could not communicate with us the way most children could. Add two more kids into the mix as well, and I confess I felt completely exhausted most of the time.

Frank, being in real estate, was often able to work from home and help out with Luca, Grace (who is two and a half years younger than Luca), and Gabriel (who is three and a half years younger than Grace). Caring for our younger children obviously required much work, but it was also a tremendous blessing that I was *able* to stay home with them, thanks to Frank's job. He could sometimes work from home, and our stable income insulated us from concerns about paying for care, food, or rent. I realize that most people are not that fortunate.

Life, however, definitely didn't look the way we thought it would look when we said our "I do's" the day of our wedding. Our daily routines, our schedules, schooling, church, our traveling, our vacations—every little detail of our lives was affected by a new normal.

I was grateful I had the privilege of spending each day caring for Luca, Grace, and Gabriel, but honestly, I didn't have much of a life outside that. Parenting is demanding, but the level of hands-on commitment it requires to be someone's caregiver takes parenting to a whole new level. I have a huge heart for caregivers. I understand what caregiving takes. Caregivers are selfless in nature, but even they need respite, or they will burn out.

I had a hard time adjusting at the start. This was not how I pictured Luca's life unfolding. This was not how I pictured our lives unfolding. But it's not as if Luca had those kinds of expectations for his life, either. He had his own challenges to navigate, just as other children would have theirs.

One of the first steps to accepting a new normal is to let your expectations go and to surrender your victim mindset. Our expectations will almost always let us down, and God owes us nothing in this life. This is a life we *get* to live. This is a life in which we *get* to love. God has gifted us *with* life. Scripture never says it will turn out the way we want it to.

In fact, quite the opposite is sometimes true. Scripture is filled with people whose well-intentioned plans fell by the wayside when God stepped in. Moses and the burning bush. Mary and her immaculate conception. Ragamuffins on the margins of society who encountered a man named Jesus.

As exhausting as it was at times being a full-time caregiver, it didn't take long for it to become my purpose, my calling. What a *blessing* that I was *gifted* with the chance to spend each day next to my little boy—to be in the very presence of an angel, God's gift to us!

As Luca grew older, I sometimes thought about that little girl who was pulled from her middle school that fateful day, whose life was uprooted, whose emotions were in turmoil as she watched her mother marry a stranger. I didn't have much of a choice then about my surroundings, but I had a choice of how I could react when I was confronted with Luca's trauma.

As difficult as accepting a new normal might be, remember that God has thousands of blessings and gifts for you within this acceptance. What matters is not meeting our expectations of how life is supposed to go, but rather how love leads us deeper into life. We can only do the best we can in the situations we've been given. What a blessing it was that God gave me the opportunity to be Luca's Mama, to partner with God in giving our children a safe home to belong—to grow up in a secure environment, to be loved unconditionally, to *thrive*.

Embracing Your Divine Assignment

Once you accept your new normal, the next step is to *embrace* your divine assignment. That divine assignment will most likely entail seasons of life that feel like a long journey through the valley. But accepting your new normal roots you in the present, not the burdens or mistakes of your past, and not the intimidating hurdles in the future. It opens your eyes to see God's love and grace in the present, even amid the fallout of past disruptions and the future mountains that have to be climbed. It opens your eyes to the opportunities God has for you *now*. It opens your eyes to the grace and joy that is to be experienced *now*, even in a complex moment of tension and unknowing.

Throughout Luca's treatments, one of my most difficult experiences as a mom was watching Luca go under anesthesia—not because I didn't trust the doctors, but because I felt helpless and unable to do anything to help him. As crazy as it is, Luca probably had to "go under" more than 150 times throughout his three cancer battles. Think about that: more than a hundred times in sixteen years.

And it never got easier for me, as his mother.

Each time, there was an excruciating uncertainty and nervousness about what was to come for our little boy. It always felt like I was being internally emptied, forced to let go and surrender him over to a surgery or treatment that would most likely leave him weak, battered, and bruised on the other side of his sleep.

One particular time, however, I remember being able to see beneath my anxiety and nervousness and instead experience a certain humor in the moment. Luca was fifteen and was being prepped to go under anesthesia. Frank and I, as always, each took a side at the head of the bed. When we saw the nurse hold the gas mask above Luca's face, I leaned close and gave him a tender kiss on his chubby, rosy cheek. Then Frank did the same on the right cheek.

To break the tension, Frank cracked a little joke: "I'd better not get too close to that gas mask because then I'll be the one falling asleep," he said.

Luca grinned.

Then Frank reached under Luca's head and placed his hand there. When the anesthesiologist placed the mask over Luca's nose and mouth, my son held his breath—and laughed. He knew that would keep him awake for at least a little longer.

Luca was being a little stinker. He was trying to see how long he could go before he went under. It wasn't the first time he'd attempted this.

"Luca, time to take a deep breath," I said. I glanced at Frank, and we both did our best not to crack up. We were drinking in this brief moment of levity, welcoming any respite from the stress of the situation.

Meanwhile, Luca was still holding his breath. In our experience, Luca normally went under in fifteen seconds. But this time, he held his breath for at least forty-five. Eventually, enough of the gas reached his lungs, and he went to sleep. When Luca was finally under, Frank removed his hand from underneath his head. Luca was under sedation, and that was our cue to leave. We walked away—yes, afraid, but also shaking our heads and grinning because of what had just transpired.

Being a relentless seeker of joy will help you to embrace your divine assignment. One of my divine assignments was to be Luca's mother and caretaker. I desperately wanted to do everything I could to cure Luca of his cancer, but his healing was ultimately beyond my control. Embracing your divine assignment entails finding moments of humor and joy beneath the difficulties.

Remember the Israelites' exodus from Egypt? One might argue their exodus began when God revealed Himself to Moses through the burning bush. After this powerful moment, Moses had a choice: he could either live in denial about what had happened, or he could lean into the truth of God's revelation to him. The choice was his. God was too kind to coerce Moses into his divine assignment. Moses had the choice to accept his new normal, which he did, and this *propelled* him into his divine assignment: liberating the Israelites from slavery in Egypt and guiding them through the wilderness toward the Promised Land to begin life anew.

We too, have a choice. If God showed up in Moses's life through something as unexpected as a burning bush, couldn't God show up in our lives in unexpected, unassuming ways? In leaning into his intimate encounter with God, in accepting His divine assignment, Moses might have endured more trials; it might have pushed him more internally to become who God made him to be; it might have involved more suffering. But partnering with God in the darkness of the valley and the nothingness of the wilderness gave his life purpose and meaning and liberated thousands of people.

My husband, Frank, comes from a full-blooded Italian family (as you might have been able to tell from the name "Giordano"). One of his family's heroes is the Italian priest and saint, Padre Pio. Pio, was a Franciscan Capuchin who lived from 1887 to 1968. He became famous for receiving the stigmata—wounds that correspond with the marks left on Jesus's crucified body, bleeding from his hands, feet, and side.

As a follower of Christ, Pio accepted his calling and his plight. He embraced his physical sufferings, the controversy that followed him, and the unique ministry he had as a stigmatist. He had a remarkable ministry and impact on others through two world wars because of his willingness to accept the life God gave to him, which included its fair share of challenges. In embracing his divine assignment, he was an encouragement and a hope to people in a dark time, when the world was in turmoil.

John Alessi's book *The Brave Little Soul* has always resonated with us because, like Pio, there was such a bravery that defined Luca's life. God inhabited Luca's beautiful heart and mind and revealed Himself to us through our son. Like an angel sent to show us the way, Luca opened our eyes to see things we had never seen within ourselves.

After Luca's first diagnosis, for example, Frank began to take steps forward in his faith like he had never done before. Faith had always been a part of his life, but Luca's trials uncovered an intimate dependency that changed him from the inside-out. Whereas faith had always been very private to Frank, I suddenly saw him comforting families at Rady's, often sitting down to listen to their stories and lift them up in prayer, there in the hospital. Luca's suffering certainly opened him up to see the sufferings of others in a deeper way.

A couple years after Luca's second diagnosis, I was drowning in exhaustion from mothering three children, yet was unable to sleep because of anxiety. My buried childhood trauma, as well as the trauma from Luca's diagnoses, had brought me to a place where I could no longer deny my need for healing. I had so much to process, so much to take to the Lord. Each day caring for Luca brought me life, joy, and laughter. His bravery as he navigated a challenging life made me brave. His joy amid his difficulties made me joyful amid mine. Spending each day with him, as I emerged from another sleepless night, breathed life into me.

Each of us has a cross that we must carry. That cross might involve incomprehensible pain, but as Jesus showed us, there might also be nothing as powerful and as healing as the cross we carry. His divine assignment saved the world. Our divine assignments can help to heal our own souls, as well as the souls around us.

Let the burning bushes in your life, the angels in your life, guide you deeper into your divine assignment. The toughest thing you have to do might end up being the best thing you ever do.

When Your Divine Assignment Changes

Luca halted and stood firm. He didn't want to move his feet. To me, he looked tired.

Stopping in the middle of a walk around our neighborhood was unlike him because of his compliant and easygoing personality. He was fifteen at the time. In the past, he had no problem keeping up with Frank or me, especially if one of us took his hand. This time around, though, he didn't want any help. He wanted to stand on the side of the road and not move forward.

Why is he doing this? I wondered. *Is there something wrong?*

Maybe he had hurt his leg. Or maybe he was focused on something; he could get a little obsessive when the moment was right. Whatever was bothering him at the time, he couldn't tell us because he didn't have the ability to express himself beyond pointing or uttering a word or two.

I noticed something else later that day, when Luca went to the bathroom. He often needed assistance, so either Frank or I would help him with his bathroom needs, but on this occasion, I was surprised to see his legs shaking when he stood up after being on the toilet. He seemed weak to me—like he'd been during our morning walk on our cul-de-sac.

When my cheek touched his on this particular evening, I made an emotional plea to the Lord: *God, we love him so much. Please let everything be all right with our precious boy.*

The next day, Frank and I noticed Luca hitting himself in the head, tapping the right side of his head with his knuckles. What was going on?

Whatever pain Luca was experiencing seemed to go away because for the next couple of days, everything seemed to go back to normal. That weekend, however, when Frank and the kids went over to his parents' house for one of his family's Sunday lunches (I was on a lunch date with a childhood friend), something else happened. Over dessert, Luca's mouth began to droop. It did the same thing later on, while they were playing ping-pong. Frank called me, and we decided it would be best that he take him to Rady's immediately, while I picked up Grace and Gabriel. Remember, it had been *eleven years* since we had seen any scares whatsoever regarding the return of Luca's cancer.

Those were anxious moments, waiting to hear from Frank. When he called to tell me that the two of them would be staying the night at Rady's, my heart sank. I knew Luca would have to have an MRI to discover if there was a serious issue. But it was late, and I wanted so desperately to bring my sweet boy home, tuck him into bed, kiss him on the cheek, and tell him I loved him.

I silently prayed a prayer of protection over Luca. He had endured so much, and he deserved only roses and sunshine for the rest of his life. Just the thought of something being wrong with him again evoked intense anger in me.

I asked Frank to put the phone to Luca's ear. Part of Luca's bedtime routine was to cuddle with me as I read a book. The first thing Luca said was, "Mama, home." My heart broke, but I choked down my emotions so I could be strong for him.

"I'm sorry, sweetie. You're going to stay in the hospital tonight with Daddy, but Mommy loves you, and I hope you sleep well. I'll see you first thing in the morning, Love Man."

That was October 30. The next day was Halloween. Part of me thought it would be nice if Grace and Gabriel could get dressed up and see their friends because I wanted things to be "normal" for them. But I didn't have it in me, and neither did they. Those days were a blur, clouded by worry.

Sometime during their night at the hospital, Frank later told me that he heard Luca say, "Daddy." There was a certain desperation or pain in his voice. It was as if he knew that whatever was happening in his body was not good. When Frank looked over, Luca was holding his hand out for Frank to grab. Frank got up from the couch and pushed a chair next to Luca's bed. Luca placed his hand in both of Frank's, and Frank caressed his hand until he fell asleep again.

Frank told me that happened several times throughout the night. Luca's soft voice would call, "Daddy," and he'd hold his hand out from his bed.

That long night at Rady's would end up being the very start of Luca's final fight with brain cancer, a fight that would eventually take his life. Though I wasn't there in the hospital room that evening, I often find myself thinking about that scene.

Whenever we find ourselves on the edge of a new normal, on the brink of accepting the next stage of our divine assignment, it can often feel scary and overwhelming. The fear and intensity of the present situation can be paralyzing. That's okay. Sometimes we have to proverbially spend the night in the hospital and be present with our pain—to sit with it and process it.

In moving toward acceptance, we must surrender. All we have is the life we've been given, and there's no sense wasting years wishing it looked different. We eventually must hold our hand out, just like Luca in the middle of the night in that hospital room, and whisper, "Daddy, Abba, Father."

Acceptance evokes surrender, and Luca can teach us a lot about a posture of surrender. He never knew what it was like to be in control. He never had that luxury. He was dependent on us for everything. He was dependent on God for everything. All of life's essentials, he needed our help with: to eat, to drink, to use the bathroom, and to get ready for bed. We tried to help foster his independence in any way we could.

My mom was really great about helping him in this regard. Whereas I always had my hands so full as a caregiver and therefore seemed to be hands-on at all times, she was great at reminding me to create space to cultivate his independence. Whenever they went out to eat, for example, she would give him money, have him go up to the counter, choose what he wanted, and pay for his own food. She always took him out to do fun and creative things that made him feel autonomous.

I think one of the reasons we struggle with surrender is because we've fooled ourselves into thinking we are the ones in control. We think our wealth or possessions or long-term security give us control, but if there's one thing COVID-19 has taught our country, it's that everything we thought was secure can be wiped away in an instant.

Like many children with special needs, Luca wasn't burdened by the things that seem to derail many people's lives: materialism, ego, or the need to climb to a certain position in the world. He simply was who he was: God's child, our child. Without having to sift through all the clutter, Luca lived a life that was animated by a contagious kind of surrender, a surrender that still inspires me today. This surrender enabled him to accept the life God had for him.

When Luca passed away several months later, not only was I overwhelmed by the level of grief I was experiencing in losing a child, something no parent should ever have to endure, but a part of my identity also began to die that day. Not only was I Luca's mother, but I was also his caregiver. Of course, I had two beautiful children yet to raise and a husband to live out life with, but the job that had kept me busy literally 24/7 was keeping Luca alive. As with any other person who pours "too much" time into their work, their job becomes who they are. If I am no longer Luca's caregiver… what am I? Who am I?

I had to learn to live without Luca's warm hugs, without the sweet things he would say, without his contagious laughter and quirky sense of humor. I had to learn to live with the fact that Luca was in a perfect place with Jesus, and he no longer needed me to help him with his daily routine. In all honesty, the routine was sometimes exhausting, yet it gave me a purpose greater than myself.

Isn't that what we all want? Don't we all want to be needed for a purpose greater than ourselves? A purpose that will outlive the number of days we have on this Earth? Our children are supposed to outlive us and carry our legacies and the memories we create together with them. They, in turn, teach their children what they learned from us. What a great honor it is to be entrusted by the Creator of the universe with such a meaningful purpose.

In the dark night of the soul that followed Luca's death, I knew I stood at a crossroads internally. Christi had passed away. Luca had passed away. My identity as Luca's caregiver had faded away. The level of grief made every day feel like a steady sinking into an ocean of despair. But each day, I also had another option. In that sinking, I could dare to hold out my hand, like Luca in that hospital room, and cry, "Daddy, Abba, Father," as Christ did in the Garden of Gethsemane. I could patiently wait for God to grab my hand, hold it in His, and let Him hold me in His arms until I fell back asleep.

Yes, my identity had changed significantly. I could no longer be a mom to Luca or a sister to Christi the way I had been before. I could still be his mom and her sister, but obviously not in the same way. It helped me to ask God what my identity in Him was. His Word says that we are saints, blessed, appreciated, saved, reconciled, afflicted, heard, gifted, new, forgiven, adopted, loved, rewarded, and victorious. God acknowledges and understands our suffering and has given us unique abilities he wants us to use in our Christian ministry, both inside the church and in our communities. He loves each of us with an everlasting love, even when our identity shifts or our divine assignment changes.

When loss swallows you, the grief process can sometimes feel like one of those intense home-improvement projects. Before you move forward, you have to knock down the walls and rip up the floors. It's brutal and exhausting. Anger is common. Force is required.

If you stick with it, you get through the demolition phase, but the house looks terrible—even worse than before. It feels like you're going backward. Sometimes the house is even unlivable. But in ripping the house up, you're creating the space to do more inner work. And that's when you have to get precise. You have to make measurements and order parts. You have to ask questions and be open to learning as you go. You can't judge yourself when you fail but instead use what you've learned to propel you forward. You have to get curious and be willing to try new things.

On the other side of it, you end up with a transformed house, but it takes so much work to get there. You can't just jump from the crucifixion to the resurrection. It's the space in between where the renovation and transformation occurs. It's often in the suffering that the transformation occurs.

Here is what God told the "brave little soul" in John Alessi's beautiful piece:

> The suffering soul unlocks the love in people's hearts much like the sun and the rain unlock the flower within the seed. I created everyone with endless love in their heart, but unfortunately, most people keep it locked up and hardly share it with anyone. They are afraid to let their love shine freely, because they are afraid of being hurt. But a suffering soul unlocks that love. I tell you this—it is the greatest miracle of all. Many souls have bravely chosen to go into the world and suffer—to unlock this love, to create this miracle—for the good of all humanity.[2]

I can still hear Luca saying, "Mama, home" to me over the phone like it was yesterday. Of course, what he meant in saying those two simple words is that he wanted to go home. But over the years, what he said has taken on new meaning for me. Luca had a way of being home wherever he was. I can say that confidently because of how joyful he always was. If he was around people whom he loved and who loved him, he was home.

Whether it's the demolition, planning, or renovating phase of building, we must never forget that where we are, no matter the state of our house, we are always home. It's home because God is there with us, coming alongside us as we bust down walls and rip up floors and invite transformation. God empowers us and animates us as we renovate. As

2. John Alessi, *The Brave Little Soul.*

Paul wrote in 1 Corinthians 6:19, "Do you not know that your bodies are temples of the Holy Spirit, who is in you, whom you have received from God? You are not your own…" Our very bodies are where God has chosen to dwell. He has chosen to make us His home, and because of this, we are never alone, even when our divine assignment changes. We are filled by the transforming reality of love.

CHAPTER 4

An Angel's Abiding

In Matthew 18:1, one of Jesus's followers asks him this question: "Who, then, is the greatest in the kingdom of heaven?" The question, as self-centered as it is, is also honest. In Luke 9, we read that the apostles are having a similar discussion—actually, an *argument*—among themselves about who the greatest is.

Many of our desires in the present day, whether we are aware or not, reflect those of the people and followers of Jesus in first-century Palestine. We want to have all the answers. We want to be on the inside. Perhaps we want to be able to judge others and feel like they are wrong and we are right, even if this desire is subconscious. Many of us build our entire lives on chasing ego boosts. In other words, we want to be recognized as the greatest. On one level, it's human. On a deeper level, it's futile.

Upon hearing the question in Matthew 18 about who the greatest is, Jesus does something counter-cultural and profound. He calls on someone nearby who has no social standing: a child. He places the child before the crowd and says, "Truly I tell you, unless you change and become like little children, you will never enter the kingdom of heaven. Therefore, whoever takes the lowly position of this child is the greatest in the kingdom of heaven. And whoever welcomes one such child in my name welcomes me" (Matt. 18:3–5).

What is it about a child that makes him or her the greatest in the kingdom of heaven? I can only speak from a parenting perspective, but when I think about children, I'm reminded of their innocent willingness to *trust* and *abide* in their parents or guardians. Again, acceptance is the beginning of surrender, but it's this steady trusting and abiding that creates a posture of love and freedom.

The importance of abiding is ingrained in our biology. From the moment a child is conceived, he or she is completely dependent on the mother—for nutrients, safety, growth, and development. The child abides in the mother. The mother is in the child, and the child is in the mother. It is a beautiful illustration of what it looks like to abide in Christ and be united with Christ. The child continues to depend on his or her parents until independence is achieved.

Whereas most children are raised to become independent, Luca remained in a childlike state because of his profound special needs. He was always dependent on us and fully abided in us to care for him and to love him. He was always open to receiving our love, our help, and our guidance. It is no wonder people described him as so loving and free.

As we each grow older, it seems that we have a harder time receiving love and opening ourselves up to help and guidance. Yet God longs to love, help, and guide us every second of every day, beckoning us deeper into His presence.

Later in that passage, in Matthew 8:10, Jesus continues, "See that you do not despise one of these little ones. For I tell you that their *angels* in heaven (emphasis mine) always see the face of my Father in heaven." In other words, children have a connection to eternity that we as adults sometimes lose touch with as we cling to the things of this world, they often live more freely than we do because of their ability to abide, and they often see a spiritual reality more clearly than we do in our obsession with accomplishing and attaining things.

One of our spiritual tasks in life is to become more like little children. To open ourselves up more and more to God's love, help, and guidance. To let go and let God, as the cliché goes. To hear our names, rise from the crowd, and naturally rest in our Savior's arms, in His sweet embrace. To see life more through a heavenly, eternal lens and perhaps, like the angels, glimpse the face of our Father in heaven in our closeness to Him and dependency on Him.

Praying Without Ceasing

Before Luca's first brain surgery, a nurse entered our hospital room. By this time, a few close friends were there, along with my mom, Lu Ann; Frank's mom, Lea; and Grace and Gabriel. We had kept the kids out of school; we needed to support each other on such an emotional day.

"I have some pre-op papers for you to sign," the nurse said. "Shall we go find a room?"

Frank turned to me, and we shared the same look. *Wow, this is going to happen.*

There is a 1 in 100,000 chance of a child under two being diagnosed with medulloblastoma in the United States each year. We had met another family that day who was in the exact same situation. This is the club that no one ever wants to join.

We were led to a consultation room, where we sat across a table from one another. Armed with black fine-point pens, we worked our way through a half-inch-thick sheaf of papers. Frank was used to reading real estate contracts for a living, so legal documents—which these were—didn't throw him. That said, we could tell we were basically signing over our son's life and agreeing not to hold Rady's responsible in the event of Luca's death. Indeed, the consent forms said as much in about eight different ways: *Your child could die, and you need to acknowledge this.*

This was the beginning of what would become a looming decade-and-a-half encounter with the reality of death. It's a grim truth that you never really grow numb to. Parents in the pediatric oncology wing understand. The risk of death is always there, haunting you like a ghost.

Most people live their lives hardly thinking about death until someone passes away, but when your child has brain cancer, you go through a certain grief cycle just because of the harsh reality you're forced to confront. A recent devotional from GriefShare, an organization that supports people as they grapple with loss, said it well: "When a person you love is sick or suffering, you begin to grieve before the actual loss. In some cases you may think that most of your grieving is already done. But despite your preparations, the grief that occurs after a person's death goes beyond all your expectations."[1]

---

1. "Day 48—Grieving Before the Loss," GriefShare, https://www.griefshare.org/dailyemails/recipients/wBJXQEP7z2LHe1U9FiX3/messages/48.

The intensity demands an emotional response, or it will all likely build up within you and be projected onto those who you love. Children wear their feelings on the outside for the world to see. They honestly react to whatever it is they are experiencing, sometimes consumed with joy, wonder, or playfulness, other times seized by anger or sadness. Good parents let their children know that the emotions they feel are a natural part of life. Their emotions are not to be suppressed. We need to validate them first, and then we can teach them how to deal with them appropriately.

It seems to me that it's only when we get older that we begin to suppress what we think and feel. Maybe this is because we had a parent or guardian who shamed us for feeling certain emotions in our childhoods. Little girls are sometimes shamed for feeling anger, whereas little boys are sometimes shamed for feeling sadness. We become self-conscious. We become hyper-aware of how we're perceived. We fear what others may think about us if we let our guard down and say what we want to say or vocalize what we really feel. We're afraid of the vulnerability that comes with "becoming like a child." Make no mistake, it really is scary! But I believe this kind of childlike vulnerability is what God invites us into. Vulnerability paves the path to abiding.

When we have the courage to be emotionally vulnerable, we open up our souls so that God can fill us with His Holy Spirit; we share the truth with God so He can meet us where we are. This kind of openness with God in our prayer lives helps us gain an awareness of what is going on within ourselves, and it invites God to permeate the deepest, darkest places within our souls. This might have been what the apostle Paul meant in his letter to the Thessalonians when he told them to "pray without ceasing"—to be in constant, honest communication with God throughout all of life, not just on the mountaintops, when we're dressed in our Sunday best, but also as we journey through the valley.

Luca taught me how to be honest and vulnerable with God and others, just as he was so honest with us. He was navigating unthinkable circumstances during his angelic mission on Earth, but, like a lot of children—especially those with special needs—he communicated with us through his emotions. He masked little, for he did not seem ashamed of anything. He lived his life with a profound acceptance of his reality, which is to say he accepted how God made him and the mission that God gave him.

It seemed like Luca was always open to experiencing joy within the present moment, *especially* when he was around others. Like any child, he simply wanted to love and be loved in return. He never fantasized about the future or allowed himself to be shackled by the past. He had no ego, no agenda. In some ways, though I know he faced unfathomable challenges, it seemed like his beautiful simplicity protected him from the anxiety we all know so well. He prayed without ceasing in his ability to be fully present—body, soul, spirit—in the moment. He was uninterested in masking shame or escaping anxiety. He epitomized the childlike faith Jesus talked about, fully abiding in the comfort of those who loved him.

That included the darkness, too. Like when he held out his hand in the middle of the night at Rady's amid his third cancer diagnosis and pleaded for Frank to hold him, there on the edge of another brutal fight for his life. Or when he came home from school one day and, in a fit of rage, began screaming and flipping our furniture over in the living room. Who knows what had happened, but my guess was that something occurred on the bus that tore him up inside. Perhaps someone had made fun of him. Or maybe the complexity of the life he was navigating weighed down on him on that particular day. We did not try to calm him down. We didn't discipline him for his anger. Our Luca had few words he could use to communicate to us, so we always—*always*—encouraged him to communicate with us through his emotions. I moved objects out of the way so he wouldn't get hurt, and, once his fit was over, I held him and comforted him.

In his book *Disappointment with God*, Philip Yancey writes, "One bold message in the Book of Job is that you can say anything to God. Throw at him your grief, your anger, your doubt, your bitterness, your betrayal, your disappointment—he can absorb them all. As often as not, spiritual giants of the Bible are shown contending with God. They prefer to go away limping, like Jacob, rather than to shut God out."[2]

To truly abide in God, we must become more like children. We must realize that God not only loves us but accepts us as we are—*all* of us, even when we are struggling, even when we are helpless and holding out our hand or hurling furniture across the living room. Through-

2. Philip Yancey, *Disappointment with God: Three Questions No One Asks Aloud* (Grand Rapids, MI: Zondervan, 1988), 263.

out the Gospel, the breadth of Jesus's emotions is constantly on full display—yes, His rich compassion and joy, but also his deep anguish (Garden of Gethsemane), anger (flipping tables in the temple), and feelings of betrayal (the crucifixion).

As Peter Scazzero wrote in his popular book *Emotionally Healthy Spirituality*, "Ignoring our emotions is turning our back on reality. Listening to our emotions ushers us into reality. And reality is where we meet God." He later concludes, "Emotions are the language of the soul. They are the cry that gives the heart a voice."[3]

Continually inviting God into our inner worlds, no matter the junk we're carrying, is to pray without ceasing. Like a child abiding in the loving arms of his or her parents, we, too, must abide in God, knowing that nothing is too much for Him, too dark for Him, too complex for Him. He runs toward us like the father in the parable of the prodigal son, in full pursuit of us, no matter what we're carrying.

Abiding in One Another

"How long will it take Luca to wake up?" I asked.

"An hour or two," said Luca's neurosurgeon, Dr. Levy, a down-to-earth and kindhearted man who always tried to make children and their families comfortable.

We were expecting to see him sooner and feared something might be wrong. Luca was fifteen. The three of us thanked Dr. Levy and his colleagues for everything they had done for our son and returned to the waiting room, where we shared the not-so-good news with our children, parents, and friends.

A short time later, Dr. Crawford, the director of Rady's neuro-oncology department, pulled Frank and me aside. He had a deflated look in his eyes.

"I spoke with Dr. Levy and his medical team," he began.

"What did they say?" Frank asked eagerly.

"Well, first, I am really pleased with the surgery. Luca could have died, but he pulled through. Dr. Levy did a fantastic job, and I'm pleased with the amount of tumor he was able to resect. We couldn't

---

3. Peter Scazerro, *Emotionally Healthy Spirituality: It's Impossible to Be Spiritually Mature, While Remaining Emotionally Immature*, updated edition (Grand Rapids, MI: Zondervan, 2006 and 2017) 49.

have asked for anything better, especially with the complications that cropped up."

Just then, a nurse entered the waiting room. "Are you Luca's parents?" she asked.

"Yes," I replied.

"I can escort you to the ICU to see your son."

Finally.

We were led to the ICU, but another nurse was waiting outside the entrance. "You're going to have to stay in the waiting room," the second nurse said.

Something wasn't right.

An hour later, another ICU nurse came out to the waiting area. She looked a bit rushed and told us that Luca was upset, screaming, and trying to disconnect himself from some of the medical equipment. She feared there might be something wrong with his brain from the operation. They needed to sedate and intubate him again to calm his hysteria.

"He'll come out soon. I'll let you know when that happens." With that, the nurse returned to the ICU.

It had been a long day. It was past nine in the evening. We asked two of our family friends to swing by the hospital to take Grace and Gabriel back home.

It wasn't until 10:30 p.m. that Frank and I were told Luca was waking up and we could see him. Even though we were mentally and physically exhausted, we both knew this was a big moment, so we gathered ourselves.

When Frank and I walked into the ICU, six doctors and nurses stood surrounding Luca. They were working on taking out his breathing tube, but they weren't having immediate success.

One of the nurses caught my eye and noticed the look of apprehension on my face. "He will be okay," she said. "This is normal. This is what some people do when they come out of surgery like this. He won't even remember this later."

After a few moments, the tube was successfully removed. A doctor said, "Come on, Luca, breathe."

I held my own breath as more doctors and nurses urged Luca to start breathing on his own. Finally, he gurgled and inhaled a breath of air into his lungs, and everyone else in the room exhaled in relief. That's when Luca looked around and saw half a dozen gowned doctors and nurses hovering over him. He suddenly started screaming, "Out! Out!" The scene was wild and chaotic.

I drew closer, and that's when I saw the huge incision that started near his right temple, traveling toward the top of his head, and then circling down the right side of his skull toward the back of his neck. The hair on the right side of his head had been shaved, but he had a full head of hair on his left side. The fresh stitches were soaked in dark red blood, and the long incision looked like a reverse question mark.

Luca's face was swollen, and there were light patches of black and blue on his skin. He looked like an eighteen-wheeler had run over him. His body had been hammered, and I found it impossible to see my child like this. My heart broke for my son. I felt both sadness and anger well up inside me—sadness because Luca had endured such a procedure and its aftermath and anger because I was helpless to do anything to make things better for him.

I gave in to my tears. While the doctors and nurses finished with Luca, a nurse beckoned me. I stepped closer to Luca's bed and sat quietly beside him, careful not to bump into anything. I just wanted to be as close as possible to my son. I leaned closer and whispered, "Mommy is here, Angel Boy. You're doing great. We're going to take care of you."

Every mother is familiar with that desperate sense of needing to know her child is okay—that desire to draw close to her child…to hold tight and never let go…to nurture her child back to health. We as parents (and, in particular, mothers) are very good at nurturing, but sometimes we struggle with opening ourselves up to being nurtured ourselves—by God and by others. When enduring the darkness of the valley, I think the human tendency is to feel like you're alone and that your situation is too much for others to handle. You feel like you're in your own little bubble and you don't want to burden anyone with your problems. Though the world keeps spinning, it feels like you're drowning.

Especially after Christi passed away months later, I struggled to find the courage to open up to others about the pain I was feeling. I felt like I was back in the ICU, trapped in a desperate space where I was crushed by Luca's horrific post-surgery state, determined to nurse him back, but all the while struggling to allow others to support or nurture me while I nurtured him. When Christi passed away, the person I had always opened up to about everything was suddenly gone.

At that exact same time, Luca was the weakest I'd ever seen him. I really needed Christi and didn't know what to do without her. I desperately needed to find someone else in my life like her—a woman to venture through life beside whom we could gift one another with the spiritual act of listening—but I felt isolated and afraid. I did what I had to do and pushed through my grief.

I knew a woman named Allison whose son had passed away, and I thought about reaching out to her. I felt that inner spiritual tug that we all know well. I needed to connect with her, but then I thought, *She lost her son; I don't want to burden her with my own struggles.* I was so wrapped up in caring for Luca and all the emotions I was navigating daily, so I kept putting it off. I have the tendency to procrastinate things in my life when I feel overwhelmed—even things that I know would be good for me.

It wasn't until months after Luca passed away that I finally reached out to her. I'm glad I did. We were able to help one another grieve as we listened to each other and shared what we had learned on our own journeys. She told me that she had been wanting to reach out to me, too.

Hunkering down or "pulling ourselves up by our bootstraps" is sometimes necessary, depending on our God-given personalities, but what we need more than anything in the long term are deep *relationships* with one another. Our individualism in our country has made us ambitious and innovative, but it has sometimes blinded us of the reality that we all need one another. We are all spiritually connected on a fundamental level. This is what the apostle Paul meant in 1 Corinthians 12:26 when he wrote about the unity and diversity within the Body of Christ: "If one part suffers, every part suffers with it; if one part is honored, every part rejoices with it."

When you injure part of your body, even a small part of your body—say, a pinky finger—you focus all your attention on the care of that specific part. Your body works to heal itself. Our bodies' many systems are interconnected, affecting one another. A body is made up of many parts, but they all make up *one* body.

The early church's unity propelled it forward. The people cared for one another and focused their attention on the part of the body that was suffering the most. Its unity positioned it to celebrate its diversity.

The church's mission was centered around *community*.

All the great stories in the Bible had this collective perspective that the early church epitomized. Angels throughout the Bible almost always helped prepare human beings for a mission that was far bigger than themselves—whether it was Moses leading the Israelites out of slavery, Mary carrying the Savior of the world in her womb, Peter basically establishing a new religion for the Jews, or Paul taking the Gospel to the Gentiles. The Bible's heroes often went on individual journeys involving spiritual revelations that ended up benefiting a larger whole.

Just as we abide in Christ and pray without ceasing, we must also abide and *confide* in one another. We weren't meant to go through this treacherous world and painful life alone. Luca helped me understand that not only did I need to depend on others, just as he depended on us; he also helped prepare me, as angels do, for a bigger purpose that involves serving those within the Body of Christ.

In caring for Luca, I learned so much about nutrition, cancer treatments, feeding tubes, and even child psychology in specially gifted children. As Christians, our ministry is to use our own unique journeys to help others in theirs. We are called to serve the Body of Christ and use our own stories to help others feel less alone.

Not long ago, for example, my friend, Maressa, called me because she needed help reinserting her daughter's feeding tube. She and her daughter were super nervous about touching the area where the feeding tube went in her tummy. Because of my journey with Luca, she knew she could reach out to me. I had twelve years of experience with feeding tubes so it was second nature. I arrived and was able to do the procedure while she observed. Now she's a pro and will be able to help someone else. I believe this is how things should work within the Body of Christ.

Thanks to how God has used our suffering to connect with one another, I have been able to go with Maressa to Rady's and visit while her daughter was a patient and lend a listening ear. I'll be honest: it's really challenging sometimes to go back into that place where so much trauma unfolded for us as a family. Sometimes I have flashbacks. Sometimes tears well up in my eyes as I'm seized by an unresolved moment that I had with my son years before.

But in the Body of Christ, we use the pain and darkness of our crucifixions to help others experience the hope of resurrection. We allow others to minister to us in our own pain and darkness. When you go through something difficult, it expands your heart (if you let it) and helps you unite with other people's suffering, just as Christ did for us.

Two months before Luca passed away, we decided to have a baptism for him in our pool. We could tell that his health was beginning to fade. We saw the writing on the wall but didn't want to believe it at the time. How could we not baptize the person who taught us more about how to truly live as a follower of Christ more than anyone we had ever known? Leading up to the celebration, Gabriel (nine at the time) approached us and asked us if he could be baptized beside his big brother. This was one of the biggest spiritual decisions he could make, and he wanted to do it with Luca—beside him, in the water.

With only a day's notice, fifty people came to witness the celebration. My dad and Frank baptized the boys. It was a beautiful picture of community and communion. Each of us has the opportunity, each day, to enter the water alongside our fellow brothers and sisters in Christ; to stand beside them; and to be transformed by God, together, as one family.

All Creation Sings

When Luca passed away, we felt the heavy loneliness that so many people feel when they are blindsided by grief. I felt like God had abandoned us. I felt like God had teased us with all the hopeful signs we received over the years of Luca's healing. I had faith, all the way up to when Luca took his last breath, that a miraculous, divine healing awaited him. God had other plans. And we were all left in the rubble of our faith. I felt lost at sea, in the middle of a dark storm, something that some might call "spiritual distress." The way I thought God would operate imploded. I had fallen into my own dark night of the soul.

Yet, in the depths of the valley, God was faithful in a new and different way. I was reminded that despite the pain I felt, I could abide in a God ,who knew what it was like to be human—a God who suffered and died a lonely death, who felt betrayed and humiliated, a God who fully understood the intricacies of my pain. I found it important to take a step back and still find gratitude for life despite my pain, cultivate wonder for life despite my worry, and name the blessings in my life despite all we had lost. That's not to downplay the real intensity of loss or slap a bandage over the importance of the grief process—but I find it equally important to not lose hope, to keep going, and as Christi said, to refuse to cave to despair.

One of the areas where I found God—or perhaps better said, where God found me—in those lonely months was nature. Blessings—divine remnants—are all around us. We just have to have the courage to open our eyes to see that God is meeting us where we are and reminding us of His truth. As we go deep into the darkness to do the hard work of grieving, wrestling, questioning, and doubting, we have to be just as willing and open to how God might find us with His light.

The night Luca passed away, we received a call from two of our good friends, John and Debbie, who had left our house thirty minutes or so before Luca had passed away. In the chaos and heaviness of the evening, John had accidentally left his phone at our house. We thought that might be what they were calling about, but it was something much deeper.

John told us that when he and Debbie had sat down in their living room after all that had unfolded that day (this would have been right around the time that Luca stepped into heaven), their dog suddenly began whining and pacing back and forth between the two of them. So John got up and went outside with their dog. In the quiet stillness of that June evening, he looked up into the clear, black sky. A strange feeling came over him, as if something out there was trying to speak to him. John was a skeptic when it came to spiritual matters. But he told us he felt something that could only be described as God's presence. He admitted to us he was freaked out by it. He stood there in the silence for ten minutes or so, both gripped and confused by what was happening. For some reason, he felt like God was inviting him into a conversation. Unsure of what to say, he prayed, "God, if Luca is with you, show us a shooting star."

Something deep within his spirit told him to look toward the direction of our house, and then heard a voice that said, "Now count down from ten."

Feeling even more insane by this point, he started counting.

Ten...nine...eight...seven...six...five...four...three...two...one.

When he reached *one*, he saw an elongated oval flash across that exact section of the sky where he felt led to gaze. The light immediately faded out, almost as if a light had been flipped on and then quickly shut off. A neighbor of theirs later confirmed seeing this same bizarre flash in the sky toward our house. It wasn't a shooting star, John said. But it was something cosmic, almost like the streaking tail of a comet that was visible only for an instant. He felt as if God was saying to him, "Luca is home."

John had been led outside by his dog, invited into prayer by the sky, and God responded to his presence with a mysterious flash near our home, as if to indicate Luca's arrival in heaven—*Luca's light.*

God's miraculous creations continued to sing.

After Luca's memorial service several days later, we followed a black hearse to a nearby park, where Luca's body and casket would be interred in a mausoleum wall. We decided to use a crypt instead of an underground burial. We just couldn't handle the idea of Luca's body being underground.

When we were making arrangements, one of the things Jerry, the mortician, asked us was whether we wanted to release white doves as part of the interment ceremony. Since the days of Jesus, the dove has represented love, peace, and purity—and has become a symbol of the Holy Spirit. When a covey of doves is released at a funeral, those who are mourning a loss are said to have "released their loved one" in a special way, which can help in the grieving process.

The way Jerry explained things, a single dove—the leader—would be released, and then another fifteen doves would be let go from a separate cage. The covey of doves would unite and fly behind the leader and then return to the trainer, where they would be put back into their cages. We decided that, yes, we wanted to do this.

Something unusual happened during the ritual. After the leader dove was let go, the other fifteen doves were released, but one dove refused to leave his cage. The trainer struggled to get him out, grabbing for him and getting more embarrassed as the mourners watched.

Finally, the dove escaped and flew into the sky, which drew a few chuckles from us. Instead of joining the rest of the doves, however, this particular dove landed on top of the twenty-foot-tall mausoleum wall, in the exact center, just above the crypt that would be home to Luca's casket. The dove could have flown anywhere or alighted in a nearby tree, but it chose to land and stay on the abutment above the place where Luca would be laid to rest.

Every dove returned to its cage—except this one. Like a sentry standing guard at the Tomb of the Unknown Soldier, this solitary white dove remained at his perch, overlooking us as we took part in the interment ceremony. For ninety minutes, the bird remained on the wall in the triple-digit heat.

Later, after everyone left, including us (the cemetery didn't allow family or friends to watch the casket being inserted into the wall), several workmen came to finish the interment.

The dove stayed on its perch above the workmen, they later told us. The moment the casket was inserted into the wall and closed off with a section of granite, the dove flew away.

"I had goosebumps," said the worker who told us this story. "I've worked here ten years, and I've never experienced this before. That child of yours must have been very special."

We had asked our friend, Gary, to capture everything that day on camera, and during the interment, he noticed the dove perched on top of the wall. He took one picture of the dove, and when he looked at the instantaneous result on the back of his digital camera, the dove had a white halo around it—the only photo out of hundreds with a halo in the picture frame.

"I can't explain it," he said.

The morning after the memorial service, at seven in the morning, a neighbor at the end of our cul-de-sac named Robin got into her car and made a short drive to the home of Tina, who lived across the street and two houses down from us.

A few months before Luca left us, the two ladies, who were both quilters, had said they wanted to make a quilt for him. We were deeply touched by the gesture. Tina had asked me what Luca's interests were.

"Oh, that's easy," I said. "Anything Disney."

So they made Luca a wonderful quilt using images from the Disney animated film, *Finding Nemo*, one of Luca's favorites. Tina, who had an embroidery machine, went the extra mile by embroidering his name and one of our favorite Bible verses on the quilt. We chose Jeremiah 29:11: "'For I know the plans I have for you,'" declares the LORD, "'plans to prosper you and not to harm you, plans to give you hope and a future.'" This verse had always encouraged our family.

These two good friends had a standing appointment to walk together every weekday, from the entrance of our cul-de-sac to the very end of our street, which is a little more than a third of a mile. The way Robin and Tina figured it, five round-trip laps equaled just under four miles, which took them about an hour to complete. While they chatted, they got their exercise for the day.

That morning, as they started walking in front of our house, Robin and Tina talked about Luca and our family. They had sat together at Shadow Mountain Church and heard all the speakers at Luca's memorial service. I remembered hugging them at the reception and thanking them again for their support and for the *Finding Nemo* quilt, which had been very meaningful.

Our street is as straight as an airport runway, but over the last seventy-five yards or so, it gradually descends into a cul-de-sac. At the very end of our street, several houses sit considerably below the elevation, including Robin's home, which is dug into the hillside. This means anyone walking to the end of our street receives an awesome view of the valley below and the foothills in the distance, without any houses in the way.

That morning, June 28, was predicted to be unseasonably cool. Instead of a high of 100 degrees, which had been the high of the previous two days, meteorologists were predicting a mild high of 83 degrees under sunny skies.

The sun was already high in the sky when Robin and Tina completed their first lap to the end of the cul-de-sac and back. In the middle of their second lap, as they descended the cul-de-sac, the oddest thing happened.

They told me that as they looked out beyond our cul-de-sac, a bed of clouds rested on the valley floor. From that pillow of stratocumulus, a white rainbow arched against a canary-blue background in the sky. The rainbow must have been several miles across, just like a regular rainbow.

White rainbows are exceedingly rare in nature and are caused by sunlight shining through droplets of water from fog. Because fog droplets are smaller than rain droplets, color is lost, and the rainbow presents itself as white.

They started back up the road toward the other end of our street, where we lived. Once the street leveled out, they both looked behind them. The white rainbow was gone. They continued walking, making their loop around the neighborhood, and no rainbow was visible throughout the rest of the neighborhood. But the second they passed our house and started descending into the end of the cul-de-sac overlooking the valley, the white rainbow reappeared!

They took two more laps, and the exact same thing happened. On their fifth lap, all they saw was a clear, blue sky. Robin and Tina sent us photos of the meteorological phenomenon and told us they couldn't help but talk and think about Luca during their walk. Four white rainbows, only to be seen from right outside our house. Luca was in heaven with the Father, Son, and Spirit.

God woke me up in those days. I was struggling and hurting, but He reminded me that I was surrounded by splendor, beauty, divine miracles, and, yes, goodness, amid my pain. Brokenness might have been part of our reality, a natural part of life, but still, I was surrounded by His love and grace, even in the middle of a storm. Creation invited me to experience His comfort. To abide in Him and to rest in Him. As Romans 1:20 says, "For since the creation of the world God's invisible qualities—his eternal power and divine nature—have been clearly seen, being understood from what has been made, so that people are without excuse."

Though our pain was a reminder that we were pilgrims journeying through this often-difficult life on Earth, the overwhelming beauty of the flashing cosmic light, doves, and white rainbow reminded us of eternity—something that we could taste and experience *while* we were journeying through the valley. The miracles He revealed to us—miracles that surrounded us every single day—gave us glimpses into a heavenly realm.

Luca had set an example on how to become like a child again. He had guided us all into a richer, more fulfilling spiritual life. He had fought the good fight—a lifetime of abiding, surrendering, loving, and blessing—and now he is forever abiding in the arms of his heavenly Father.

CHAPTER 5

An Angel's Light

In the second chapter of Luke, we read about shepherds who were going about their daily routine, taking care of their flock in the quiet stillness of the evening. It was then, we're told, that an angel of the Lord suddenly appeared to them, bursting into the peacefulness of the night with a radiant light.

Imagine how startling that must have been. Imagine their terror and shock as they were blindsided by the supernatural. This might've been the equivalent of working in your office and suddenly seeing the walls in your building come crashing down.

But the first thing the angel said to the frightened shepherds was, "Fear not" (Luke 1:13, KJV). This message isn't new. Over and over again, around four hundred times, the Bible commands us not to fear. In this story, God let the shepherds know that He was on their side—and He continues to let us know that He is on ours. It's as if God is constantly trying to tell us that we are not alone and that, because of this reality, we have nothing to fear.

You probably know the rest of the story…the Christmas story. Once the angel calmed the shepherds, he made them aware of the miracle that took place in Bethlehem that night: the birth of our Lord and Savior, Jesus Christ, the long-awaited Messiah. Just as the magi went on a long journey to witness the birth of their Savior, following the bright star in the sky over the far-off, unassuming town of Bethlehem, the shepherds, too, responded to the angel's call and journeyed to witness this divine birth. Both allowed the light in the sky on that dark night to guide them, to witness the birth of a miracle that would change the world, to experience the prophetic fulfillment of the Messiah. On the journey through fear, into the unknown, into the mystery of the night, they followed the light.

I recently typed "Luca Giordano" into a Google search bar. Nothing came up. There was no mention of him winning a tennis tournament or kicking the winning goal at a San Diego Surf Cup soccer tournament. He never had a Facebook or Instagram account until after his passing. Because he didn't leave a digital footprint, no one outside his family, close friends and acquaintances would ever know anything about him. But to those of us who knew him the old-fashioned way—in person—Luca was the strongest, most loving sixteen-year-old we had ever known. He had the ability to bring countless people closer to God because of his animating light and joy.

It was evident that the Holy Spirit dwelled within him and gave him the courage and strength he needed. He couldn't help but exude joy, even during unimaginable circumstances. When I'm having a frustrating day, when I'm feeling the weight of fear or anxiety, I am reminded that I can do all things through Christ, who gives me strength. I had the best role model in Luca. He was and will always be my hero.

Anxiety runs rampant in our society, and whether or not an individual has experienced traumatic events, he or she will most likely deal with it at some point in life. I have learned that when you feel anxious, it is important to ask God what He says about your current situation. As Philippians 4:6–7 says, "Do not be anxious about anything, but in every situation, by prayer and petition, with thanksgiving, present your requests to God. And the peace of God, which transcends all understanding, will guard your hearts and your minds in Christ Jesus."

Peace is what we all want, really. Our Lord and Savior, Jesus Christ, imparts His peace to us. He gives to us what the world cannot. Like the angel and the star in the Christmas story, Luca was a light that guided me deeper into my faith and a spiritual world—to encounter the miracles that God has for us when we have the courage to listen to His call and follow the light. Luca has guided me through fear, despair, and uncertainty to witness where joy, hope, love, and peace—the light of Christmas—might be born in the far-off, Bethlehem corners of my interior world and life.

Nonno Beppe, Luca and Daddy, 2002

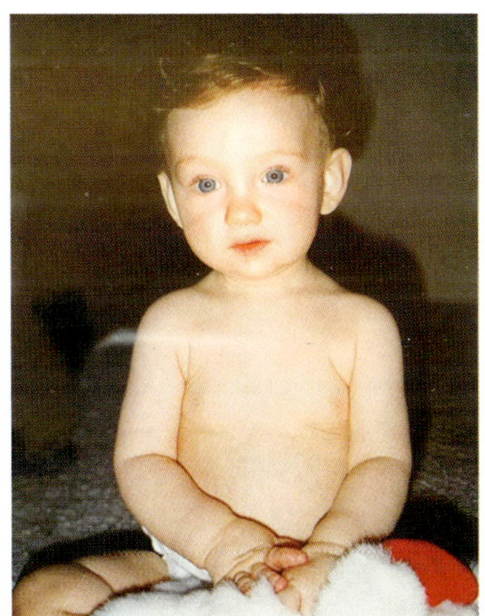

My angel baby

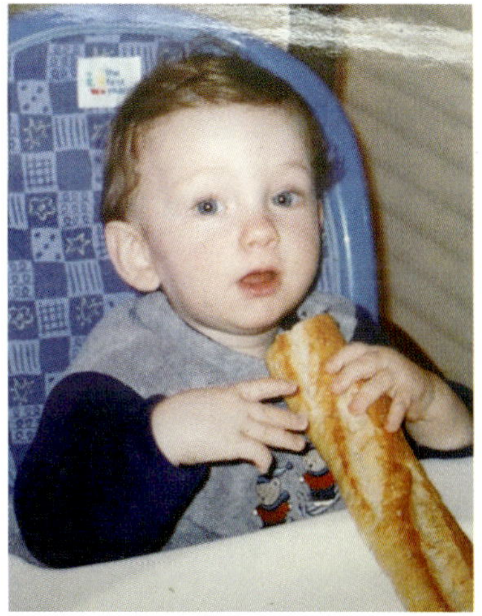

Luca loved his Italian bread

Luca and Grace, Christmas 2005

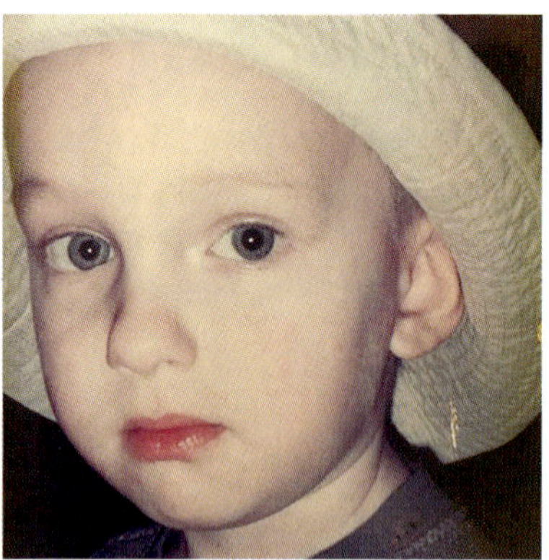

Luca in one of his many hats

Christmas 2009 - Frank, Elena, Gabriel (2), Luca (8) and Grace (6)

Luca, 18 months, just before his first diagnosis

During treatment, after first diagnosis

Giordano family, 2012

Luca with Grandad's OU hat

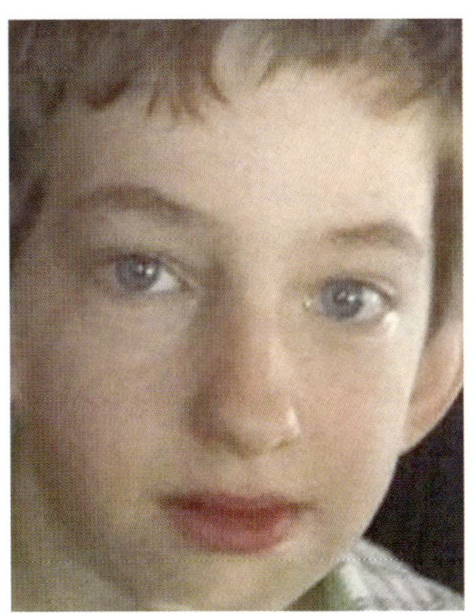

Those eyes

Gabriel and Luca at Balboa Park

Ready for school, 2013

Giordano family, 2015

Brothers, 2015

Luca's 8th grade harbor cruise

The Three Musketeers

Cousins hanging out – Travis, Jesse, Grace, Luca and Gabriel

Luca's 15th birthday

Luca loved to swim

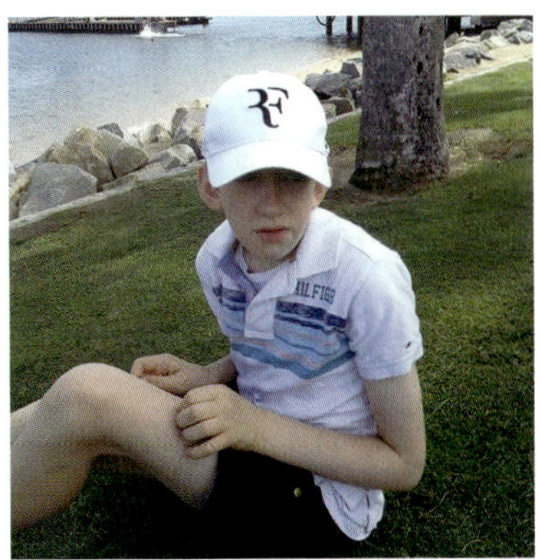

Luca in Coronado

Grammy, Elena and the kids

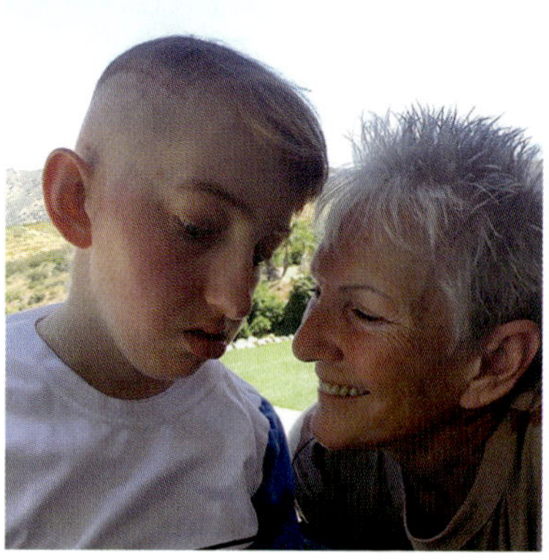

Grammy and Luca, 2017

Luca's Make a Wish trip to Disneyland

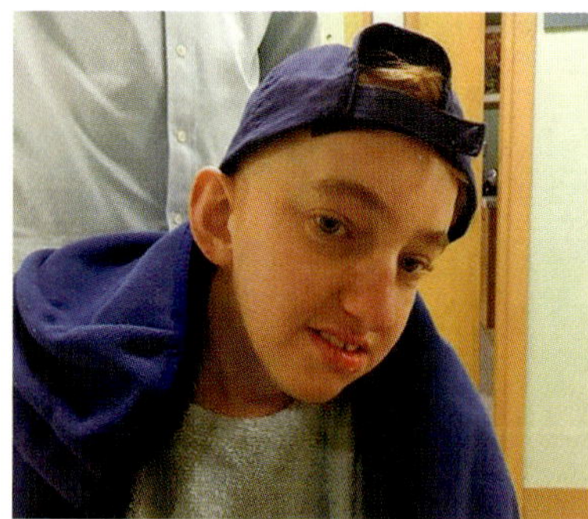

Luca after a round of immunotherapy at Rady Children's Hospital

Luca dancing with his dear Nonna

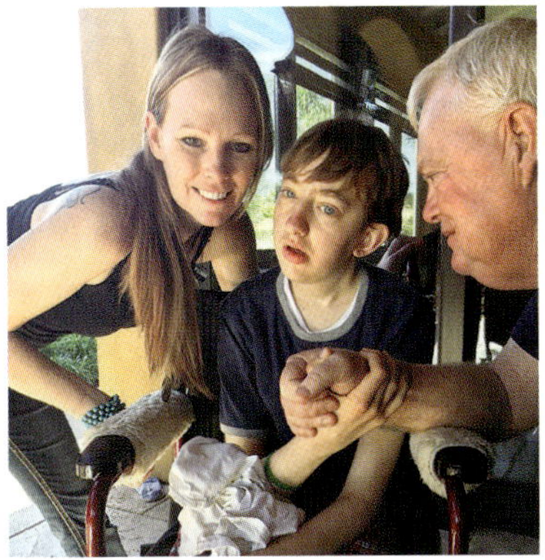
Christi, Luca and Grandad

Christi and Elena - Best friends

Giordano family, 2017

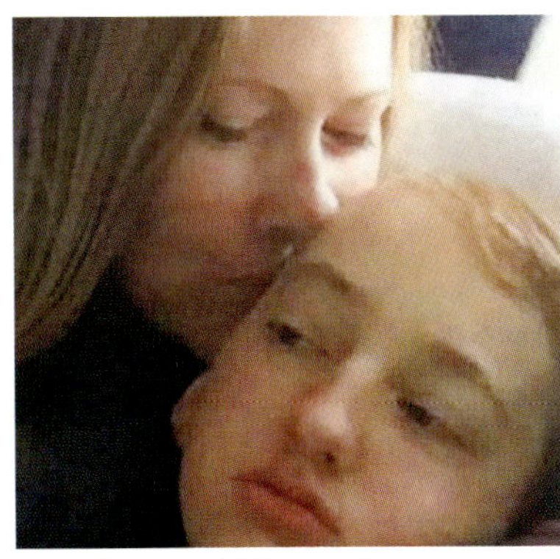
Luca cuddling with mom

Daddy and Luca on the buddy-bike

Daddy with the kids

Luca and mom enjoying a meal at True Food Kitchen

Gabriel helping at Luca's Light fundraiser

Luca's Light fundraiser with Dr. Crawford, Dr. Levy, and grandparents

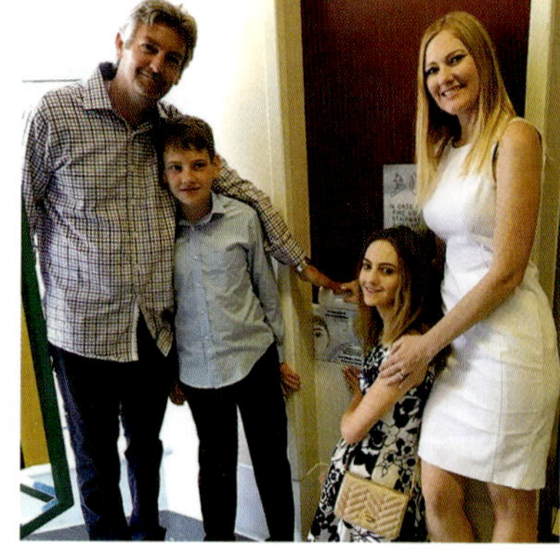

Our family after placing Luca's memory tile at Rady Children's Hospital

The Choice We All Have

A few months after Luca turned sixteen, a nurse and parent liaison at Rady's handed us a brochure for the Make-A-Wish Foundation, which makes life-changing wishes come true for children with critical illnesses. Make-A-Wish creates joyful experiences for children and families who are enduring unimaginable circumstances. This brings a profound sense of hope to children, families, and communities. This hope cultivates transformation, sometimes even empowering a child to fight an illness with more vigor and families to overcome their despair. That's what hope does—it transforms.

She handed this to us at a difficult time in our journey. Luca had turned sixteen not long before, and we feared then that it would be his last birthday we'd celebrate. A sixteenth birthday is a traditional rite of passage. It's the year most young people get their driver's license and experience the first whiffs of freedom, but none of that was going to happen with our son. Instead, we had a low-key birthday celebration at our home and invited a few family members and close friends to come over after church. We presented Luca with a small cake with a single candle in the center, and we all sang "Happy Birthday" as he curled up on the couch in the family room. His body was struggling. He was fatigued.

We wanted to enjoy the day, but it was such a sad time. The only thing we really had to be thankful for was that the proton therapy treatments had ended. We were confident the radiation was keeping the tumor at bay, but we were also aware of the chance that the tumor would grow again. That's what Dr. Crawford had been warning us to expect.

When the nurse handed us the Make-A-Wish brochure, Frank and I both felt reluctant. We didn't want to take funding from another deserving family. In fact, we had donated to Make-A-Wish in the past. But the more I thought about it, the more I felt like it was something we should at least submit. I helped Frank see that this worthwhile organization was formed for families like ours and had special connections to provide experiences we wouldn't ordinarily get if we tried to do them on our own.

So, the next day, we filled out the form on the brochure and sent it in. One of the questions was, "What is the child's wish?"

We chose the Happiest Place on Earth. Luca loved Disneyland. We usually drove to the Magic Kingdom in Anaheim once a year and had a blast every time. Within a few days, we were contacted by a nice woman from the San Diego Make-A-Wish chapter.

"Would your son like to go to Disney World since he's been to Disneyland?" she asked.

We felt it would be too much for Luca to fly, so we declined her generous offer. "We also want to be close to Rady's in case something happens and we need to get him back there," I added.

"Okay, Disneyland it will be."

When we told Luca we were going to Disneyland, his eyes lit up. "Dinnyland!" he squealed with joy. A fancy white limo bus came to our home to pick us up. At four in the afternoon, we were dropped off at Disney's Grand Californian Hotel inside the California Adventure Park.

Disney representatives were on hand to greet us. There was no red carpet, but there might as well have been one. Everything was handled as we were shown to our lodging—a suite with several bedrooms. Luca was given a blue Make-A-Wish T-shirt and a black Make-A-Wish hat, along with an "Aladdin" lanyard, which was like a key to the city—it could get us anywhere. We could tell that he felt special and valued and that he knew this was different than our other trips to Disneyland.

First was the Disney California Adventure Park. The Aladdin pass allowed Luca to bypass lines and go on rides again and again—anything he wanted. I'll never forget how attentive Gabriel was to his brother. He pushed him everywhere in his wheelchair and sat next to Luca on as many rides as he could. They especially enjoyed "Soarin' Over California" and pretending they were Lightning McQueen or Mater on the "Radiator Springs Racers" ride. (Luca was a huge fan of the animated film *Cars*; he loved to watch it over and over on his iPad.) When we finished the ride, a Disney "cast member" asked Luca if he wanted to do it again.

Luca nodded, and off we went…over and over.

The next morning was our day at Disneyland. Because of his wheelchair, as well as his physical condition, we couldn't do the "big rides" like the Indiana Jones Adventure, Splash Mountain, or the Matterhorn Bobsleds, but we did get him on Pirates of the Caribbean and Thunder Mountain, which had some pretty good dips. We also did a lot of kiddie rides like It's a Small World, Mad Tea Party, Dumbo, and Mr.

Toad's Wild Ride. The highlight was a special visit with Mickey Mouse at City Hall near the Disneyland entrance. Luca tried to pull his nose off, which Mickey handled with complete poise.

We spent a second night at the Grand Californian Hotel and had the run of the park for a third day. We were grateful for everything Make-A-Wish did behind the scenes to give our family an incredible adventure.

Luca would pass away a few months later, but I still catch myself smiling whenever I reflect on those days at Disneyland with Luca. We knew his situation was bleak. Perhaps *he* knew his situation was bleak. But Make-A-Wish positioned all of us to bask in the joy of the present moment, to escape the darkness for a bit, and to simply enjoy watching our son be consumed with wonder and awe at his favorite place on Earth.

Make-A-Wish and Luca were a perfect fit because that's what Luca did throughout his life: he chose light, even in the grimmest of circumstances. As he fought for his life, he laughed with the doctors and nurses. He befriended other children at the hospital. He had constant fun in the very place where all his trauma had unfolded. He made memories. He had the remarkable ability to live in the present and enjoy God's grace, however it was being revealed in any particular moment of his life. Through family. Through friends. Through playing with our dog, Max. Through rewatching a movie on his iPad. He drowned out fear with presence and joy; and, in doing so, he taught us all how we're meant to live.

Luca treated every day like "Dinnyland."

Each of us has a choice in this life: to be a negative person or a positive person, to be a force of darkness or a force of light. The world is negative enough as it is, dark enough as it is, broken enough as it is. What it needs is *light*...kindness, joy, hope, love, and peace. As Anne Frank wrote, "Look at how a single candle can both defy and define the darkness."

God has blessed us with free will. We each get to choose what kind of attitude, perspective, and mindset we want to adopt. When life caves in on us, when adversity pierces through our carefully crafted armor, our true colors are revealed.

Each time we received the news that Luca had cancer, we knew we had a choice: we could cave to fear and adopt a "woe is me" attitude or believe the angel's words in the Christmas story, "Fear not," and trust that the light would mysteriously guide us forward. We had to trust that as difficult as the journey might become, we were not alone.

It's our journeys through the darkness, paradoxically, where we have the potential to become a light for others. After all, what made the angel in the Christmas story so trustworthy? It was the fact that the angel had heavenly insight on the happenings of that night. In our own darkness, we have the opportunity to gain heavenly insight—knowledge for the deepest layers of life like suffering and love—so we can then come alongside others in grief and suffering, mirroring what God does for us.

What is the evidence of God's grace in your life today? What are the miracles unfolding before your very eyes? What's the light you can name in the dark?

Keep Your Eyes on the Light

The hours passed slowly. They'd told us Luca's surgery would take around four hours, and at four o'clock, my anxiety level began to heighten. It was our first time going through the anxiety of having a child in surgery, and it was among the most dangerous surgeries in modern medicine.

Every hour or so, I called the phone number that connected me with a nurse next to the operating room. We really appreciated their communication, though we were probably a nuisance. It was just a really vulnerable period of waiting. We were terrified that we might lose our toddler in such a serious surgery. Each time I called, the nurse gracefully delivered the same message: "Surgery's going well. He's stable." In other words, *He's still alive, but that's all I'm authorized to say.*

Luca was not quite two years old. He had been diagnosed one week before his second birthday. And his tiny skull was being torn open to carefully remove a massive tumor.

Two of our dear family friends arrived with deli sandwiches from their favorite Italian delicatessen as the waiting continued. We waited and waited until 6:30 in the evening, when we received a page. That meant we were supposed to call the number we'd been given.

The nurse told us that Luca's surgery was over and that we could go to the consultation room off the operating room—the same room where we'd signed his life away. "Dr. Levy's getting washed up. He'll meet you there," the nurse said.

Six and a half hours for the procedure! I wondered what that meant and decided it could be taken two ways:

They needed all that time to remove every last cancer cell from his brain or *the operation went on so long because they ran into problems.*

When Frank's mother realized the procedure was over, she slid up next to him.

"*Posso venire con te?*" she whispered. *Can I go with you?*

"*Sicuro,*" Frank replied. *Sure. Of course.* He figured we could get away with bringing one more family member with us.

The three of us found our way to the consultation room and waited for Dr. Levy to appear. We didn't have to wait long. When he opened the door, my mother rushed him like an outside linebacker and grabbed his hands.

"Did you get it all? Is Luca okay? How did it go? How did it go?"

Frank looked Dr. Levy straight in the face and tried to read him. He appeared more solemn than usual. Was that a bad sign?

Dr. Levy wiped his brow with the back of his hand. "Well, I got most of it," he said.

"Dr. Levy," Frank cut in, "you said most of it?"

"Yes, and by that, I mean I got 98 percent of it out. There was a little bit left, but I just couldn't get it out without doing damage to the brain."

He said the mass (medulloblastoma) was gray in color, and most of it was encapsulated, but the part that was attached to brain tissue was difficult to remove.

I was too stunned to say anything. None of us spoke up as we contemplated what this meant for Luca's future.

"But you know," he finally said, "even if there's a little bit left, I'm really happy with how the surgery turned out. We did an MRI toward the end, and it looks like we got it out—except for that little bit. This tumor was in an incredibly difficult part of the brain to reach."

That was perhaps the moment when we realized Luca would have a long road ahead. We were told that, though the surgery was overall successful, damage was likely done to his brain that would hinder his development. Not only that, but a very small part of the tumor was still there, making us wonder if the cancer had indeed been eradicated. That lengthy, six-and-a-half hour waiting period during Luca's surgery represented what our lives would become. No idea how to plan for his future. No idea what effect this challenging brain surgery would have on him. No idea if he'd ever know what it was like to be a "normal" kid.

Venturing through the valley will inevitably involve long periods of helpless, torturous waiting. These desert phases are where it is most difficult to discover joy. Returning to the Christmas story, think about how long the Israelites had awaited their long-promised Messiah. Yet it is not our job to obsess over the future. It's our job to discover joy in the present. In 1 Peter 1:8–9, the apostle Peter writes to fellow Christians who had never met Jesus, "Though you have not seen him, you love him; and even though you do not see him now, you believe in him and are filled with an inexpressible and glorious joy, for you are receiving the end result of your faith, the salvation of your souls."

We were grateful that Luca continued to progress in physical therapy. Looking back at our long periods of waiting during Luca's complications, what we're most thankful for is that we found *joy* in spending time with our son.

One of the books I read after Luca's death was *Wonder* by R. J. Palacio, which was made into a movie that was released in November 2017, just five months after Luca died. The film was an adaptation of an endearing book about a fifth-grader named Auggie who had a medical condition that left him with a disfigured face. While Auggie wasn't dealing with a life-threatening disease, there were cute moments of interaction between him and his parents that reminded us of Luca. The message of the book and movie was *kindness.*

Auggie, despite his plight—his classmates' teasing and bullying, along with lacking self-worth and experiencing shame about something that was not his fault—was a light for others in the movie, most notably his best friend, Jack Will. Auggie taught Jack what was most important in life and planted a seed for kindness among his peers and at his school that would later grow into a beautiful garden. Auggie's embrace of his own journey—his relentless commitment to being kind, no matter how mean everyone else was—inspired his classmates on their own journey toward kindness.

Wonder might have been fiction, but it resonates because we're all familiar with the story. The person on the outside looking in—the one who is most misunderstood and most different—often holds the key to our own awakening. Those people are the lights that help us to become who we are supposed to become, the angels that guide us forward so we might witness the miracles of life, where love is born.

In the Christmas story, we witness the birth of a Savior who was born into an oppressed group that was under the boot of the Roman empire, in something so unassuming as a stable, in something as dirty as a manger, where the animals fed. His ministry echoed these same notions. He constantly gravitated toward those on the outside—those who had been pushed out by society, those whom the religious elite had ostracized. Jesus was not the kind of light the Jewish people expected Him to be. Instead of a conquering king, he was a suffering Savior. But He was the light the *world* needed— and He still remains that light of the world today.

As you journey through the valley, look for the light in the unassuming places, in the uncomfortable places, in the places where Jesus might have been born, where He might have shown up riding on a donkey, where He might have healed a leper or met with a woman at a well. Those are the places where God might teach you something new and light up your heart, mind, and soul in an unexpected way.

For Jack Will, it was Auggie. For me, it was Luca. It was impossible for Luca to understand the gravity of his situation—a small blessing, perhaps—but for us, it was often difficult to understand why this was happening to our son and to see him suffering the way he did. Have you ever been broken to the core as you watched someone you love navigate difficult circumstances? Yet, as Luca's mother and caregiver, it was his light that kept me going.

When I was depressed with the heaviness of his diagnosis, I looked forward to cuddling on the couch with him as he watched *Ratatouille*. When I was waiting for the left side of his body to heal, I held him in my arms and got lost in his captivating blue eyes. When I was wrestling with God about why my son had to face more trials in sixteen years than most face in a lifetime, I looked forward to making him smile on our walk around the neighborhood. He was a reminder to me that no matter how bad things became, I couldn't let my candle burn out.

As with Auggie, it was hope and joy that kept Luca going all those years. His ability to hope and to choose joy made it more accessible for all of us. The divine gifts we unearth in our own fights with despair often become the gifts we share with others, and that was certainly the case with Luca. I have no idea if Luca was ever tempted to fold to despair, but I'd imagine that he was. Sometimes, as I've mentioned, his anger would erupt. Sometimes he could not stop crying. He had his low moments, but he did not make despair his resting place. He always returned to joy. He could not contain it, and it emanated from him.

Luca's unique ability to focus on the light is what made him a light to others. We become what we focus on and how we think about those things. As Paul wrote to the Philippians in Philippians 4:8, "Finally, brothers and sisters, whatever is true, whatever is noble, whatever is right, whatever is pure, whatever is lovely, whatever is admirable—if anything is excellent or praiseworthy—think about such things."

Luca helped us discover that even in the middle of impossible situations, we can trust in God's ultimate goodness—that there is an ever-accessible joy beneath it all. It's up to us whether or not we dare to see it. The pain we experienced then and still experience today has brought us a closeness with God that we might not have otherwise known. Amid our grief and uncertainty, I know God to be good and personal. I know He loves Luca and our entire family. Little by little, He has shown me that death is not the end.

Light Lives On

After Luca passed away, a friend gave me the book *Daring to Hope* by Katie Davis Majors. This quote resonated with me, and it became something of an anchor of hope for me: "A watching world might say, why hope for life in a world of death? And we know the answer. This world is not all there is. And death is not the end. Our fight is not for this life. Our fight is for eternity and a hope for eternity truly cannot disappoint."[1]

Those were words I needed to read because for the last eight months of his life, Luca had not been able to walk. He'd gradually lost his ability to speak or even say a single word. That had to have been frustrating for him; I could tell he wanted to say more. What we saw in his last few months was the flowering of a young man who thought that was how life was, and he seemed to be content with it. What never changed was the constant smile on his face and his peaceful nature.

I hope I will have the same attitude the rest of my life. I'm aware

1. Katie Davis Majors, *Daring to Hope: Finding God's Goodness in the Broken and the Beautiful* (New York: Penguin Random House LLC, 2017) 83.

that my days are numbered, but thanks to Luca, I know with complete certainty that there is eternal life with Jesus. Heaven will be a beautiful place, and God and His promises are very real. Throughout the tragedies Luca endured, God's presence through His Holy Spirit has been a comfort to me. His Word has been an encouragement to me, and I have taken His strength and made it my own.

The following passage in 2 Timothy 2:11–13 has greatly encouraged me: "If we died with him, we will also live with him; if we endure, we will also reign with him. If we disown him, he will also disown us; if we are faithless, he remains faithful, for he cannot disown himself."

Scripture says that if we endure hardship, we will reign with Him. Luca endured more hardship than anyone I have ever known. No matter what this world throws at us, God's Word speaks to eternal life and the wonderful gift of salvation we all have if we accept Jesus as our Savior.

One of our neighbors told us that one evening, at about 10:30, she felt compelled to go outside. This was not a normal occurrence for her; she had been routinely winding down and watching television before bed, but she went out anyway to catch some fresh air. She told us that she sat on the edge of her spa and looked out at the valley below our houses. Then she glanced upward into the thick darkness at the shimmering stars above—and that's when she saw a long, extended white light streak across the sky. It looked a little like a meteor, but it wasn't that. It looked a little like a shooting star, but it wasn't that. Whatever it was, the celestial event was captivating to watch.

We hadn't talked in a couple weeks, so she had no idea that when she witnessed this cosmic display, it was actually right after Luca had taken his last breaths. At Luca's memorial service, John, who lived just south of all of us, mentioned that he had witnessed a similar heavenly light show toward the north that night. They had seen the same thing.

I believe it was Luca's light, outlining the path of his safe journey to heaven.

Now that light lives on through each of us. And the light of those who fought the good fight before you live on through you. This is even true neurologically. The memories of our loved ones leave unique imprints on our brains and therefore affect how we live, love, and serve. We carry the memories of our loved ones with us and have an opportunity to shine for others the way they shone for us—to let their legacies live on through how we live *our* lives, to light up a heavenly path like that star in the sky, for others to be inspired by and follow.

CHAPTER 6

An Angel's Hope

In Genesis 21, we read about the birth of Abraham and Sarah's son, Isaac, and the continued drama between Sarah and Hagar. God had promised Abraham and Sarah a son, but Sarah had long since grown beyond childbearing age, and she had given up hope. In the frustration of her own barrenness, Sarah had encouraged Abraham to take their servant, Hagar, as a second wife. Hagar bore Abraham a son named Ishmael, and they formed a strong, intimate bond, making Sarah jealous of their relationship.

In Ishmael's teenage years, Sarah and Abraham miraculously had a son in their old age, Isaac, and the drama between Sarah and Hagar returned. Sarah pressured Abraham to banish Hagar and Ishmael into the wilderness—a customary practice in that day for the son of a "concubine"—and to make sure Ishmael had no access to Abraham's inheritance as an heir.

Scholars believed Hagar got lost in the wilderness, causing them to run out of water. Hagar became afraid that this was where her and Ishmael's journey through life had come to an end. She sheltered Ishmael under some bushes to protect him from the heat and began to sob, thinking, "I cannot watch the boy die" (Gen. 21:16).

That's when we are told that an angel met Hagar where she was.

The next three verses read, "God heard the boy crying, and the angel of God called to Hagar from heaven and said to her, 'What is the matter, Hagar? Do not be afraid; God has heard the boy crying as he lies there. Lift the boy up and take him by the hand, for I will make him into a great nation.' Then God opened her eyes and she saw a well of water. So she went and filled the skin with water and gave the boy a drink" (Gen 21:17–19).

Do not be afraid; God has heard the boy crying as he lies there.

Each time Luca was diagnosed with brain cancer, it felt like our family had been kicked out into the wilderness. We probably felt something similar to what Hagar felt. What would happen to our boy? Would he survive this? Did God hear Luca's cries? Did God notice our anguish?

Over and over again, God met us where we were. He assured us that He heard Luca's cries and would not abandon us in our grief. God proverbially opened our eyes to see a well of living water that would give us the hope and the strength to take care of both Luca and ourselves in the wilderness. So much of the spiritual journey is about returning to the well and daring to hope, again and again. God taught us through Luca that we did not have to be afraid, that He heard our cries, that we were not alone, and that we could therefore have hope as we journeyed through the wilderness.

An Anchor and an Anthem

The San Diego-based rock band, Switchfoot, on the final title track of their album *Where the Light Shines Through*, sang that hope is an "anthem" of their souls. We all need anchors and anthems of hope.

An anchor centers you in place despite shifting seas and makes sure you aren't tossed about in the wind and tides. Without an anchor, the ship that is your life might be broken against the rocky shore by the slightest storm. You can find yourself frustrated and confused by the waves, unsure of what happened or where to go, constantly shipwrecked on shore or forced to start your journey over again.

An anthem is a song of the soul, calling you forward. Whereas an *anchor* stabilizes you in the storms of life, an *anthem* keeps your heart and mind focused on truth. Your anthem enables you to fight off lies from the devil and temptations of the world. Your anthem helps you abide by the warning that you "do not conform to the patterns of this world" but instead are being "transformed by the renewing of your mind," as Romans 12:2 says.

An anchor keeps your spirit centered, but an anthem keeps your soul in motion.

Luca naturally developed his own anchors and anthems. Children with special needs can teach us so much about what is most important for our own mental health. One of his anchors was his routine, as I've mentioned. No matter how tumultuous his day, he always implemented his routine, especially at night. I think it helped him feel like he had some sense of control, despite the complicated life he was tasked with living.

We often make our lives more complicated in our overthinking and obsessing. Routines can help to recenter us and reacquaint us with the spiritual rhythms of life. When I first started to invest time in self-care practices, I remember how helpful it was for me to commit myself to taking a three-mile walk in our hilly neighborhood most days and several relaxing baths with essential oils each week.

These disciplines became a venue for prayer. I was overwhelmed with mothering and caregiving—more so when my insomnia was full-blown—but I committed myself to these disciplines, even when I didn't have the energy to walk the hills. I knew from experience that I would feel better after I did. As I've heard it said, when you don't feel like praying is when you need to pray the most.

As for anthems, joy was Luca's anthem; hope was ours. They fueled one another. No matter how bleak his situation, Luca was always open to being surprised by joy from the front seat of life. You could see this in his amusement and intrigue with just about everything. Hope is essentially always being open to believing in and imagining a better life, world, and reality.

Our anchors and anthems can change and evolve, as we grow and as our seasons of life change. What's most important is that as we sail on the sea of life, we never leave shore without an anchor on our boats and an anthem in our hearts.

When Luca was diagnosed for the third time, in the shock of it all, my anchor was my kids, and my anthem was prayer. Though I was struggling to sleep and to quiet my busy mind, one thing that helped was praying each evening with Grace and Gabriel while Luca was in the hospital. There is something about the closeness of family at a trying time that brings with it a feeling of peace.

The three of us would meet in Gabriel's room, and Grace and I would sit with Gabriel on his bed. We held hands and prayed that

Luca would feel calm and that God would give him and our family the strength we needed. *And that His will would be done.*

I had learned early on with Luca that I couldn't pray for exactly what I wanted and expect just that. God wasn't a genie in the sky, ready to grant wishes. He had His plans for Luca's life, as well as ours. His plans were always for our good, even if we didn't understand them. Praying that His will would be done was freeing in a sense; it helped me accept our family's reality and surrender my fears and consuming desire for the outcome I wanted.

One evening after praying with them, when Luca had been admitted into the hospital (we'd find out his cancer had returned the following day), I still had more to process. My heart was still heavy. My mind was still busy. So I implemented another one of my spiritual recentering practices: journaling. Journaling is a discipline that cultivates introspection and honesty. It forces you to find the words to name the complicated fears, emotions, and questions that are swirling around within your mind and soul.

What I find is that in daring to be authentic and to name the truth of what I'm feeling, I often arrive at profound spiritual truths that were there all along. It seems paradoxical, but when I journal and name the darkness of what I'm feeling, I usually stumble upon the light. That evening, I penned these words:

> October 30, 2016
>
> Lord Jesus, please give our family peace during this time of uncertainty. You know our every thought and anxiety, and You alone are our Comforter. Please wrap Your loving arms around Luca, and give him strength for each day. Please work through the doctors and nurses who help Luca, and give us clear answers so we know what to do next. We don't know Your plan, Lord, but we do know that You give us hope and a future. We love You, and we trust in You.

And then I wrote down these Scriptures, reminding my heart and mind of truth in the storm. I hope they are helpful for you today:

> "You will keep in perfect peace those whose minds are stead-

fast, because they trust in you."
—Isaiah 26:3

"Cast all your anxiety on him because he cares for you."
—1 Peter 5:7

"Peace I leave with you; my peace I give you. I do not give to you as the world gives. Do not let your hearts be troubled and do not be afraid."
—John 14:27

"Let the peace of Christ rule in your hearts, since as members of one body you were called to peace. And be thankful."
—Colossians 3:15

"And the peace of God, which transcends all understanding, will guard your hearts and your minds in Christ Jesus."
—Philippians 4:7

"The LORD gives strength to his people; the LORD blesses his people with peace."
—Psalm 29:11

Scripture is the ultimate anchor and anthem. As 2 Timothy 3:16–17 says, "All Scripture is God-breathed and is useful for teaching, rebuking, correcting and training in righteousness, so that the servant of God may be thoroughly equipped for every good work." Hebrews 4:12 tells us, "the word of God is alive and active."

Scripture brings perspective to our situation, reminds us of our solidarity with the Body of Christ, and helps us refine our heavenly lenses. Scripture—God's love letter to us—keeps us moving forward and animated by hope. It reminds us of our closeness to God, even in the chaos of an unfolding storm.

A Flame in the Winds of Fear

One night, Frank was staying at Rady's with Luca right after his devastating third diagnosis when a nurse dropped by to check in on our son. This was during a time when we were weighing all kinds of complicated options regarding what the next best steps were for us to take with Luca. She listened to Frank voice concerns about Luca enduring radiation again. Luca had to go through forty-five radiation treatments each time he was diagnosed. Forty-five more following his third diagnosis would total 135 treatments.

"Dr. Crawford said it was likely that his brain cancer came back because of the radiation he had before, so I'm having a tough time deciding what to do," Frank told the nurse. "He made it clear that radiation likely won't cure our son but will extend his life by a matter of months."

"Have you heard of proton radiation?" she asked.

We had heard of it from TV advertisements but didn't know much about it.

Proton therapy, she said, used the large, heavy elements inside the nucleus of an atom to deliver its cancer-killing energy. "I know this because I'm working one day a week at the Scripps Proton Therapy Center near UCSD," she said. "Dr. Andrew Chang heads it up. People come from all over the United States, Canada, and other parts of the world to do this treatment. Perhaps it would be worth trying."

Frank spent the night in Luca's room, catnapping in a chair, waking often as he contemplated what to do about Luca. When I arrived early the next morning after taking the kids to school, we said our good-byes, and Frank excused himself. He needed to go home, grab a shower, and get some work done.

He took the elevator to the ground floor and was stepping out of the building when he realized he'd forgotten the keys to his truck. He trudged back to the elevator bay. Three doctors had stepped into one of the elevators and were waiting for the door to close. One saw him approaching and reached out to hold the door open. For a quick second, Frank wondered if he should wait and take the next elevator, but in his groggy state, he told me he decided to invade their space and ride up with them.

Two of the doctors were in traditional white lab coats and wore their identification lanyards; the third physician had a stethoscope around his neck but was wearing a Marvel polo shirt with an action figure on the front.

As Frank stepped in and turned his back to the trio of doctors, they resumed a conversation they had undoubtedly started before his arrival.

"What's the diagnosis?" one doctor asked.

"Glioblastoma," said another.

Frank said their conversation stopped there. Frank sensed they didn't want to say more because he was in their midst. He found what they said to be highly interesting; he was left with a distinct feeling they were talking about Luca.

Frank stepped off the elevator and marched back to Luca's room. The doctors walked in the opposite direction.

I was surprised to see Frank. "You're back—"

"Forgot my keys. It's one of those days," he said.

He gave me a good-bye kiss and was heading out of the hospital room when the doctor with the Marvel polo shirt walked in, followed by the two other doctors from the elevator ride. The casually dressed doctor was a young-looking Asian-American man with a buzz cut and round glasses. He looked to be in his mid-thirties. He put his hand out to introduce himself.

"I'm Dr. Chang," he said.

I noticed that Frank did a double take.

"The proton radiation doctor?"

I wondered how Frank knew who he was. Then again, considering the amount of research Frank always did, I wasn't all that surprised.

"Yes. How did you know?"

"Because one of your nurses told me about you last night. Why are you here?"

"We just had a Tumor Board meeting and discussed Luca. I thought I'd drop by and see if we could talk."

"Of course," Frank said, and he introduced me to him.

Dr. Chang consulted his notes. "I've taken some time to look at your son's medical history, and I'm confident that proton radiation can work in Luca's case. This type of treatment isn't for every patient, but in his situation, I think he could see excellent results."

Frank and I both noticed that Dr. Chang was wearing a gold earring in the lobe of his left ear—shaped in the form of a cross. Dr. Chang must have noticed that one of us spotted the cross, which explains what he said next: "Is it okay if I pray for you guys and for Luca?"

Wow. He didn't have to ask twice.

"Absolutely," Frank said.

Dr. Chang held our hands, and a prayer circle formed: the three doctors, Frank, and me.

"Lord, we stand humbly before You today and ask that You guide this family on what the best treatment would be for their son, Luca," Dr. Chang prayed. "We place everything in Your hands and seek Your direction on what to do. Lord, this is serious, and we pray for the welfare of this boy. We humbly ask that You heal him, and if our team can help in that, we pray that You would guide our steps as well. We pray this in the name of our Lord Jesus Christ. Amen."

Frank looked over at me, and I was wiping away tears. What Dr. Chang had done by praying—in a hospital setting, of all places—was giving me a tremendous amount of hope.

Seeing and *savoring* these moments of connection with others as you journey through the valley are really important in developing gratitude for the blessings of life, even in all its brokenness and flaws. Dr. Crawford writes in the afterword of this book that we, as humans, are all like molecules bouncing off one another. It's the task of the Christian to notice these divine collisions and to take note of the inner workings within the body of Christ. This work of grace helps free us from our despair.

Community sustains the soul. Relationships recharge our resolve. Together our prayers keep the flame of hope alive in a world that tries to convince us to cower to fear. As Andy Dufresne said in *Shawshank Redemption*, "Hope is a good thing, maybe the best of things, and no good thing ever dies."

Hope is an eternal flame. My flame had weathered many winds and storms, but I strived to partner with God and keep it lit. I believed, in my darkness, that somehow God would not allow that glowing flame to be completely blown out. I reminded myself that God sustained my family and me each day. No matter how desperate things became for Luca in his brutal fight, somewhere deep inside me, God placed the audacity to hope. My feelings seemed to be pure foolishness in a world of death, but God said He had chosen the foolish things of the world to confound the wise and bring about His purpose.

As we journey through the valley of the shadow of death—where the winds of fear try to quench our inner flame of hope and leave us feeling frightened and alone—we must rely on God and one another. When an expert in the law asked Jesus what the "greatest commandment in the Law," Jesus replied, "Love the Lord your God with all your heart and with all your soul and with all your mind.'" Then he added that the second greatest commandment is to "love your neighbor as yourself" (see Matthew 22:35–39).

That tells us relationships are of utmost importance to us on our spiritual journeys. Like the prayer circle that Dr. Chang formed in that hospital room, hope is what binds us together and strengthens us so we can face the invading darkness head-on.

A Present Peace and Eternal Reality

Not one of us is exempt to living in this broken reality. Each of us will be blindsided by hardship. Each of us will have to make long journeys through life's valleys. Each of us will be forced to grieve and let go. No matter what you are journeying through, each of us is also assigned with the spiritual task of keeping the flame of hope alive within our hearts.

Our world is broken, but every moment of every day, God offers us a peace that surpasses all understanding. We are not citizens of this world, so we do not need to place our identity in worldly things. As Paul writes in Philippians 3:20–21 (NLT), "We are citizens of heaven, where the Lord Jesus Christ lives. And we are eagerly waiting for him to return as our Savior. He will take our weak mortal bodies and change them into glorious bodies like his own, using the same power with which he will bring everything under his control."

We can be comforted that this world is not our home. Brokenness is not the end. Death does not have the final say. The promise of heaven for those who love God is the most hopeful gift we could ever receive. As John Bunyan described in his iconic book *The Pilgrim's Progress*, we are simply pilgrims passing through. The best thing about this life is that it prepares us for the next life.

We must use our heavenly confidence to fan the flame of hope as we walk a Christ-honoring journey here on earth. As Paul wrote in Philippians 3:14, "I press on toward the goal to win the prize for which God has called me heavenward in Christ Jesus." Our flame of hope helps us to press on even in our weakness and focus on what is ahead. It opens our eyes to the light of the present.

Hope kept us going all those years. When we began to realize that the worst thing that could possibly happen—our deep-seated fear of losing Luca—would paradoxically be the best thing that could ever happen for him, we began to uncover a peace in the present that allowed us to celebrate the highs; press on through the lows; and savor the laughs, smiles, and squeals that breathed life into our souls every single day.

All our lives are collections of moments…some dark, some hopeful. Through it all, Frank and I have chosen to cling to the hopeful moments, and we encourage our children to do the same.

I'll remember Luca bursting out laughing when a nurse walked into his hospital room without a care in the world, promptly tripped over something, and took a tumble. I'll remember when physical therapists got the left side of Luca's body functioning again after ten months of therapy and the thrill in Luca's eyes as he rode his Wiggle Racer tricycle around on his third birthday. I'll remember when doctors told us Luca was cancer-free and we all drove to Coronado Island for a celebratory lunch and a walk around the water; we crossed the Coronado Bay Bridge that spanned the San Diego harbor, and Luca would say, "Beach, beach!"—a simple word that became one of his favorite expressions.

I'll remember the balloon release at his official remission party at Grammy and Poppy's house, as each person said something they were thankful for then released their balloon into the sky—technicolored prayers of gratitude becoming speckles as they climbed into the heavens.

I'll remember every little thing from Luca's eleven years of blissful remission, from our evening routines to the enjoyment of the holidays, like when we went to Big Bear one Christmas and bundled our three children up with woolen hats and mittens so they could go sledding for the first time. Luca laughed uncontrollably as he soared down the snow-covered hill in his sled, then screamed "More, more!" right when he got to the bottom. That was Luca: fully present, addicted to joy, always wanting to extract as much fun from an experience as possible.

I'll remember the summer days Luca spent in one of his favorite places—the pool—egging his brother and sister on to splash each other or knock each other off an inflated pink flamingo or inflated doughnut. That was Luca: always intrigued with the people he loved, his curiosity fueling his enjoyment.

I'll remember his innocence and guilelessness—like the time we passed through a buffet line at a San Diego restaurant and he reached back and grabbed food off the plate of a stranger who was behind us in line. I'll remember the time Nonna showed Luca a picture of his great-grandfather, an elderly man from the Old Country complete with a scraggly beard, and Luca ran up to an old man in a wheelchair in the restaurant foyer and threw his arms around the old man's neck (practically knocking him over). Then he started tugging on the man's shirt, as if to pull him out of the wheelchair and to say, "Where have you been?"

Because God lives in us and through us, I believe every moment of our lives can be loaded with beauty and depth, and therefore with hope. The scenes of our lives are conduits for hope. And the hope we carry will help us to make the most of this pilgrimage until we pass on through to our home, united with those we love.

CHAPTER 7

An Angel's Love

Throughout Scripture, we see God use His angels to accomplish a wide range of His purposes, from something as straightforward as telling His followers to "fear not"...to something as obscure as wrestling with Jacob throughout the night. From something as momentous as appearing to Mary and shockingly informing her that she, a virgin, was pregnant with the Savior of the world...to the mystery of guiding the Israelites with a cloud by day and pillar of fire by night, deeper into nowhere.

One of the most hopeful angel accounts in Scripture takes place after Jesus's crucifixion. In the last chapter of his Gospel, the apostle, Luke, provides us with one of these examples. Luke tells us that "on the first day of the week, very early in the morning, the women took the spices they had prepared and went to the tomb" (Luke 24:1) of Jesus. That was when the women discovered that the stone had been rolled away and that Jesus's body was not there. Other Gospel writers mention that they were afraid their dear friend's body had been stolen.

But then, we are told that "two men in clothes that gleamed like lightning"—angels—appeared to the women. Luke writes, "In their fright the women bowed down with their faces to the ground, but the men said to them, 'Why do you look for the living among the dead?'" (See Luke 24:4–5).

This question rings out to us as well in our own darkness of grief and loss. Remember, Jesus's apostles and followers had no idea that He would rise from the dead. Though there are signs in Jesus's teachings of a coming resurrection, no one knew what this meant. Jesus often talked in cryptic parables and riddles. Days after His crucifixion, Jesus's apostles were smack-dab in the middle of the grief process, coping with the reality that their best friend, teacher, and spiritual guide had been brutally tortured, humiliated, and murdered, right before their very eyes.

The angel's question not only inspires the visiting women to consider a different reality beyond the final say of death; it also begs us to place our hope in this same reality of love and to realize that death does not have the final say for us or our loved ones and that there is a grounding of divine love that we stand on, even in our pain. We read that the angels continue speaking to the women who visited Jesus's tomb: "He is not here; he has risen! Remember how he told you, while he was still with you in Galilee: 'The Son of Man must be delivered over to the hands of sinners, be crucified and on the third day be raised again.' Then they remembered his words" (Luke 24:6–8).

In the angel's words, the map of Christ's love is laid out for us: to suffer, to die, and to rise again. Jesus lived fully, suffered fully, and died an excruciating death, yet death did not have the final say. We are to live similarly. We must accept our lives as they are and be unafraid to find the face of love in the depths of our suffering, dying to ourselves, and resting in hope (resurrection) amid the pain.

I have never known anyone who has done this quite like Luca. Though some might have looked at him and felt bad for him because of his lifelong fight with brain cancer and his special needs, Luca accepted the life that God gave him—and he accepted it fully. In accepting his life fully, he lived abundantly. He experienced our love for him and continued to *give* his love—to Frank, to Grace, to Gabriel, to me, to his grandparents, to close friends, to doctors and nurses—as he met deep pain and suffering head-on. He did not try to avoid it. He never became a victim of his circumstance. He fought until the very end because that's what "angel boys" and "love men" do—they want to fulfill every single aspect of their divine assignment. No matter what he was going through, Luca always seemed to "gleam like lightning."

As agents of love, we are to do the same.At Luca's memorial service, Joanne, a nurse and our parent liaison since the beginning, summarized Luca's legacy quite beautifully: "It was as if he had lived all his life *up*, loving and smiling, until he just couldn't hold on any longer." She then read a poem that she had written for him, inspired by a poem a father had written for his daughter at Rady's. It went like this:

Sweet child entrusted to our care—
Your world consisted of hospital walls and chemotherapy,
And still, you taught us.

You taught us that joy is possible
Even as our tears flow.

You taught us that strength is not of the body,
But of the mind, spirit, and gentle soul.
That time is not something to measure,
But something to cherish.

You taught us that winning isn't when you finish,
But doing the best you can with each step you take.

You taught us that faith, hope, and love will carry us,
And the greatest of these is love.

Sweet Luca entrusted to our care,
We are so very blessed by the lessons you've shared.

Life, Death, Resurrection

I was lying next to Luca on the bed in the office, the bed he'd been sleeping on for the previous eight months because he didn't have enough strength to walk up the stairs. He had become so weak that we now had a home nurse named Kim with us full time to help make Luca comfortable in his final days. Suddenly, Luca fell over. Frank and I tried to prop him up, with Kim's help. He was sixteen then, and it was difficult to move him, especially because he had no strength left and couldn't help us. I decided to sit behind him and let him rest his head on my chest. Never had we seen him this weak before.

Earlier that day, Kim had suggested that we stop feeding him since he was in a comatose state and unable to digest food. This was difficult to accept because I had been feeding him through a tube since he was four. Although I struggled, deep down, I knew she was right. With everything we had, we wanted to keep fighting for him, but we had to accept the reality of the situation. We knew he was slowing down.

For four days, Luca had spent 80 percent of the time sleeping. But we still thought he had a few weeks. His decline had been slow. On this day, however, we saw Luca take a turn for the worse. We were closely monitoring his heart rate, which was fluctuating and at one point became undetectable. He began to lose the pink color in his cheeks.

I caressed his face. "You're okay. Mommy loves you. If you need to go and be with Jesus, it's okay."

"It's his time," Kim said.

And then my son stopped breathing.

I could see life leave him. He was on his way to be with the angels.

At that moment, everything was a blur.

Frank suddenly felt prompted by the Holy Spirit to get as close as he could to Luca. He felt like God said to him, *Go to your son and tell him you love him! Do it this very moment.* Frank leaned in close to his face and said, "Daddy loves you so much. Always know that I love you with all my heart."

In my mind's eye, I could see Jesus extending His hand to Luca and bringing him into eternal glory.

That was when a miracle happened—Luca started breathing again!

The pulse oximeter showed a heartbeat. He had blood pressure.

If I hadn't known any better, I would've said that he had come back to life. More than that, I'd say that we witnessed an absolute miracle.

The hospice nurse said she had never seen anything like it.

This was another gift we had been given from God, and we wanted to take advantage of whatever extra time we had left with him. There were loved ones who had not been able to say their good-byes, so we quickly called them. Within the hour, a steady stream of family and close friends arrived to see Luca one last time. Everyone took the opportunity to express their love to him.

Luca was not in any distress. He was not in any pain. He was at peace.

As family members and visitors spent some time with Luca, Kim suddenly said, "You see how your dog is acting?"

"What do you mean?" Frank asked.

So much had been happening that I hadn't noticed that Max, our

Vizsla, had plopped himself on the edge of Luca's bed and nuzzled his nose on his legs.

"When I first got here this morning, your dog was running around, playing with people," she said. "Now Max won't leave Luca's side. He's been here for the last hour."

"When dogs do that, they sense that a loved one is going to pass on," Kim continued in a low voice. "They're very attentive. I think what's happening is that the Holy Spirit is in this room, and God is assembling His angels to take Luca home."

The majesty of the moment grabbed me by the throat. Luca may have led a very simple life, but he had one thing many of us don't—a closeness to God. As I have mentioned, when Jesus said in Matthew 19:14, "Let the little children come to me, and do not hinder them, for the kingdom of heaven belongs to such as these," He was speaking of a child like Luca.

I continued to lie next to Luca with my eyes closed, stroking his hair. Around Luca's neck was a gray travel pillow—the U-shaped kind you see passengers wearing on long-haul flights. A breathing mask was wrapped around his nose and mouth. He looked to be at peace. Every five or ten seconds, the concentrator switched on to deliver another whiff of oxygen. Frank got down beside Luca.

"Luca," Frank said, with tear-filled eyes, "Mommy and Daddy are with you, and we just wanted to tell you a few things. Luca, I love you very much. The very moment you were born was one of the happiest days of my life. You're our first child. You are a beautiful, beautiful boy. An angel. I just want to tell you that I love you with all my heart, and I always will. We'll see you again one day, when the Lord takes us to heaven to be with you. It's going to be beautiful. It's a million times better than Disneyland. We'll be praying for you every day to Jesus, and you'll be looking down on us. We'll be thinking about you every moment.

"I'll miss holding you and giving you hugs. We have a lot of beautiful memories, and I'm looking forward to seeing you again one day in heaven and seeing you do all the things that you couldn't do here, Luca. You'll be able to run and play and say everything you want to say. One day, when I'm up there, you'll tell me so many things.

"I just want to tell you, buddy, that I know it was a rough life, and you've been a fighter through it all. You're my hero forever.

"I will miss you so much until we see you again."

I was barely hanging on during this emotional moment, but I knew my son needed to hear from me.

"Luca, I couldn't have asked for a sweeter, more joyful boy," I said. "You made me a mom. I'm so thankful that I got to spend each day with you, taking care of you and loving you. You taught me about what's important in life.

"I don't think I can bear losing you, but I do have faith that I will see you again. Heaven will be so much better for you. It will be impossible for me not to see you every day, but it's going to be a lot better for you. It's okay to go be with Jesus. I love you, I don't want you to have to suffer anymore."

We really wanted Luca to know that it was okay for him to go. He didn't need to fight for life anymore. I'd heard of situations in which those on their deathbeds fought valiantly to hang on, but in doing so merely prolonged the inevitable. Luca had fought the good fight. He could go and be with Jesus.

The vigil continued for a couple more hours. Around nine o'clock, Kim slowly moved the oxygen mask off Luca's face and placed it on his chest so he could still get a little air. His oxygen levels dipped, but he was still breathing okay. He wasn't struggling to get air. He was in peace.

Right around ten o'clock that night, his breathing became very faint. His pulse rate weakened even further. Several months before, Frank had tucked a card under his pillow, and now I took it out. On it was a painting of Jesus and paraphrased verses from the book of Matthew. Holding the card, Frank read to him: "Come to me, all you who labor and are burdened, and I will give you rest, and learn from me, for I am gentle and humble of heart. Your soul will find rest."

Then Luca's eyes opened—eyes that had been shut for the majority of several days. He looked up at me and Frank with his beautiful blue eyes, but I don't think he really knew who we were. And then we saw the light disappear from his eyes.

"Go be with Jesus, Luca. He's waiting for you," Frank whispered.

This time, he wasn't coming back.

I saw that he was at peace. He had not struggled in any way. God gave us, and him, a peaceful death. Luca had a happy look on his face, and that gave me a sense of calmness about what had just happened. I felt like the Holy Spirit had given us everything we needed, as well as a reminder that there is, truly, a God. His presence was so strong, so comforting.

I leaned over and kissed Luca's forehead.

At ten minutes after ten, Luca discovered that heaven is for real.

Even in his final hours on Earth, Luca reminded all of us to fight for those we love. I have a feeling that he miraculously stepped back into his body after his heart had stopped beating—even though he was on heaven's doorstep, even though he was on the brink of leaving his bodily pain behind, even though perhaps God gave him the choice to step into the next life if he so desired—just so more family could say good-bye to him. Luca was selfless like that.

Nothing was more important to Luca than being with others, than relationships, than love. The life he lived epitomized Jesus's main commands to us—to love God and to love others. Maybe one of the blessings God gave him amid all his hardships was the ability to never get too consumed in the world—in what people thought about him, in his successes or failures, in his strengths or insecurities. As is the case with many children who are specially gifted, Luca seemed to inherently understand that he was who he was—a beloved child of God—and that he had nothing to prove. As I've mentioned, he simply wanted to love and be loved.

Regarding his three bouts with brain cancer, my feeling is that he, yes, fought for himself, but he also fought for us. His body came incredibly close to death with the treatment for each of his fights with cancer. The chemicals compromised him. Yet he kept fighting, I like to think, because of his relationships with others.

Not one of us is exempt from being blindsided throughout our lives. Because we live in a broken world, each of us will receive that haunting phone call, experience heartbreak, uncover a crushing lie, or be forced to say good-bye too soon. When life knocks us down, though, may we live like Luca, even when it feels like everything is falling apart.

We were not placed on this Earth to craft the perfect life and get everything we want. Simply put, we were placed on this Earth to be in *relationship* with God and with one another. Life has a way of emptying us and shaking us to the core, but may we, like Luca, remember those we love in our moments of weakness, and, if nothing else, keep fighting for them. Life is about relationships. In relationships we have life.

The Lamb

By now, you know Luca's limitations with communication. But as is the case with the most profound people you meet in life, their actions speak way louder than words. Here I've been, writing a book of words, just trying my best to describe Luca's inspirational actions.

Ever since Frank's intimate encounter with God that evening after Luca was first diagnosed, when the magnet with the quote from St. Francis de Sales and Psalm 27:14 mysteriously fell from the refrigerator, Frank began wearing a necklace with a gold cross. It reminded him to keep Christ at the forefront of his heart at all times.

Luca loved this cross, too. There were many times when Luca and I would be sitting on the couch, and Frank would join us. Luca would often lean over, reach for Frank's necklace, and kiss the gold cross. I recall this happening more than a dozen times. Though Luca could not recite the Sinner's Prayer, read the Bible, or sing the words of a worship song, his constant display of devotion to this cross really did make us wonder if Luca understood something of what the cross represented. Perhaps he understood it more than any of us.

Each time he did this, I was moved to try to do the same with my life—to humbly bow my head and kiss the cross.

Actions like these from Luca often helped me recenter my heart and mind. I had some really dark days during Luca's childhood. I mentioned earlier that I had insomnia and went almost three months without sleeping more than an hour or two a night. What I didn't mention is that there were moments of weakness when I looked at Frank and told him that I wished God would just take me. The trauma I'd experienced throughout my life had resulted in chronic anxiety and depression, and though cancer wasn't attacking my body like it was Luca's, I often felt just as weak. I didn't even feel human during those days. I felt like a ghost, hollowly existing.

I didn't understand why Luca was going through this. I didn't understand why my body was being affected the way it was when I had never experienced it before. My situation became so unbearable that I had to begin taking antidepressant medication, even though up until then, I had been very much against the very idea of doing so. I felt like something was deeply wrong with me. I felt so isolated that rescue felt impossible. Yet in my weakness, unsure of what else to do, I would cling to the cross.

The cross that Luca would always kiss is much more than a pendant, though that's what our culture has turned it into. The cross that Jesus died on was a torture device. To die on a cross was to not only suffer an excruciating death but also to be shamed and humiliated in front of the entire city. Jesus was abused and mocked—they called him the "king of the Jews" and placed on His head a crown of thorns. As Paul writes in Philippians 2:7–8, Jesus "made himself nothing by taking the very nature of a servant, being made in human likeness. And being found in appearance as a man, he humbled himself by becoming obedient to death—even death on a cross!"

As I believe Luca understood in his own precious way, the cross is a symbol of love. The world made the cross into an object of torture and shame, but even God redeemed that. God became lowly for *us*. He suffered and died for *us*, "for God so loved the world that he gave his one and only son." He left his heavenly home for *us and* demonstrated how to live, serve, suffer, and die through the life of Jesus Christ.

All for us.

Paul says in Philippians 3:10–11, "I want to know Christ—yes, to know the power of his resurrection and participation in his sufferings, becoming like him in his death, and so, somehow, attaining to the resurrection from the dead."

It's in our suffering that we often experience a closeness with God that we haven't experienced before. It's in our suffering that we often discover a deeper form of love. Christ suffers in us and through us, and in becoming like him in dying to ourselves, we experience a mysterious kind of divine resurrection.

That is not to attempt to explain or gloss over our suffering. I don't know why Luca had to suffer the way he did. I don't know why my body was weakened to such frailty during that trying phase of my life. I don't know why evil exists in this world. I don't know why bad things happen to good people and good things happen to bad people. But I do know that in proverbially bowing and kissing the cross in our suffering—which is to say that we dare to experience something *redemptive* within our darkness—we can begin to identify with the self-emptying of Jesus Christ.

Our suffering is not in vain. Luca's suffering was not in vain. In our suffering, we participate in a deeper spiritual reality. We encounter love. We kiss the cross.

The Lion and the Lamb

At Luca's memorial, one of the most moving moments for us as parents was when our daughter, Grace, sang Francesca Battistelli's "Holy Spirit." Our daughter is a phenomenal singer. We have seen her sing the national anthem effortlessly in front of tens of thousands of people at a Padres baseball game. But she was understandably nervous to sing at her brother's memorial, afraid she wouldn't be able to hold it together. Later, she told us that halfway through the song, all the memories of Luca hit her like a wave—his wonderful laugh, his long lashes that framed his gorgeous blue eyes perfectly, and even the way he smelled. We saw tears run down her face, as her voice became wobbly. But she kept singing. As Christi always said, she kept going.

Perhaps you've heard the song, but the chorus is a beautiful prayer to the Holy Spirit, inviting God to fill the place and for us to become aware of God's presence. This is really what all of life is about: becoming more aware of a presence that never fails.

Following Grace's song, several speakers relayed their tributes, including Dr. John Crawford (Luca's doctor), Kim Moen (Luca's nurse), and John (our neighbor who witnessed the cosmic display the night Luca passed). My father, Jim Paine, also spoke. With a preacher's heart, he said, "Luca was able to tear the barriers down to bring people to the feet of Jesus and draw them closer to Him. I tell you that Luca, in his short life, brought more people closer to Jesus than I ever have. I honor him today."

Then Jim told a story that echoed the message of the song Grace sang, a story we had never heard before. He said he had been in our den moments before Luca had passed away, and, just before Luca's final breath, he had seen a vision.

"This may blow away some of your doctrines," he said, "but Jesus showed me a great Lion from the tribe of Judah in the room. He said to me, 'The Lion is in the room,' and two lines of angels formed a receiving line, all waiting eagerly for Luca."

We were shocked.

There were many, many times in his life when Luca tried to tell us there was a lion in the room—a lion that only he could see. There had been occasions when he'd be in the family room or his bedroom, and I'd catch him looking above the door or toward one of the room's corners and ceiling. And then he'd make the sound of a roaring lion—

as in, *roarrr!*

"You see something, Luca?" I'd ask. I'd thought he was just acting funny, which he often did.

"Roarrr! Roarrr!"

Then he'd get on his tippy toes and reach up, like he wanted to touch what he saw above him. Of course, we couldn't see anything, but he was all excited, jumping up and down and exclaiming, "*Roarrr!*"

We couldn't figure out what he was trying to tell us, which happened often with Luca because he had difficulty articulating what he was thinking. One time, after he'd "seen" a lion in one of the ceiling corners in the family room, I found a book of animals and started flipping through the pages. When I found a picture of a lion with a great mane, Luca stopped me and became very animated. Then my son roared again.

Grace witnessed the interchange. She and Gabriel had worked out their own form of communication with Luca. Grace would extend her arms and make a pair of fists, and then ask Luca to tap on her right hand if the answer was yes and on her left hand if the answer was no.

In the past, for instance, she'd say to Luca, "Do you want to go out to eat? Tap yes or no."

And Luca would tap her right hand to signify yes.

"Do you want to go to the beach?"

Once again, he tapped her right hand.

To make sure he wasn't gaming the system, Grace would reverse her hands: right was no, and left was yes. Once again, she'd ask him if he wanted sliders, his favorite, or to go to the beach. He was consistent in his answers whenever she switched things around.

On this occasion, Grace told Luca to tap her right hand if the answer was yes.

Luca nodded. He understood.

"Did you see a lion?"

Luca tapped her right hand to signal yes.

We could never figure out why Luca "roared" so much in the last few months of his life. But after hearing my dad share this story, the pieces fell into place. Luca, in his childlike way, had seen the "Lion of Judah"—one of the names for Jesus Christ in the Bible.

The lion has long been viewed as a symbol of strength and boldness. Aslan, the allegorical Christ figure in C. S. Lewis's *Chronicles of Narnia*, is a lion. Christ is fully human, the spotless Lamb that was slain, a suffering Savior who we can fully identify with in our own suffering, but also fully God, the King of the universe, the one who sits on the heavenly throne.

We view lions as the kings and queens of the animal kingdom—courageous and in control. In Scripture, Christ is often called "the Lion of the tribe of Judah." When our lives are centered in love, as Luca's was, there is an underlying strength, no matter how dark our circumstance, no matter how weak we feel. Luca suffered tremendously in his life, but the way he suffered is what made him strong.

As a Christian, I believe each of us possesses an inherent boldness, strength, power, and confidence. Luca taught me that even though his body was weak in the world's eyes as he battled brain cancer, his body was much more than that—it was a beautiful temple for the Holy Spirit.

In Colossians 1:27, Paul writes about how God used the Gentiles, an unlikely people-group considering the Jews had always been God's chosen people, to reveal the truth about our union with Christ: "To them God has chosen to make known among the Gentiles the glorious riches of this mystery, which is Christ in you, the hope of glory." Luca, an unlikely character in God's divine plan, a child with special needs and brain cancer, revealed to us the riches of this oneness, which was Christ in us, the hope of glory.

Most of us have not dared to tap into the potential of what it truly means to be a dwelling place for the Holy Spirit. Most of us have not dared to unleash the inner lion—the boldness, strength, power, and confidence that resides within us when we strive to love like Christ loved us. But Luca did.

It's no wonder Luca saw lions. He lived like the maker of the universe really did dwell within the temple of his body. Angels throughout the Bible bring heavenly insight to Earth, and that's essentially what Luca did. He was animated by the power of the Lion's love, all the way up to his final breaths.

As Grace sang that day at his memorial, "Holy Spirit, you are welcome here." Luca's legacy reminds me to pray this prayer every day. To become more aware, each day, of His presence; no matter what I'm navigating, grieving, or journeying through; no matter if my present circumstance mirrors Christ's passion, death, or resurrection. May those who have loved you, those who have gone before you, inspire you to open your eyes to the lion in the room. To exclaim, "*Roarrr! Roarrr!*" when we're asked that pivotal spiritual question:

What do you see?

Epilogue

After the one-year anniversary of Luca's passing, we decided it might be good for us to get away as a family. It had been a heavy fifteen months of grief and struggle. Perhaps a vacation would help us move forward. So we went to Maui for a week with our good friends, John, Debbie, and Katrina. The trip was good for our grief. Sometimes traveling can help remove you from the day-to-day and unlock new levels of healing.

One evening, we drove to Mama's Fish House for dinner. There was a wait for our table, so we decided to take some family pictures on a small beach in front of the restaurant until our name was called.

As we walked on the picturesque beach, I thought about how much I missed Luca. He *loved* family vacations. I also thought about how much Christi would have adored this setting. So I found a stick and carved the names Luca and Christi in the tightly packed, beige sand.

After that poignant moment, we headed back to Mama's Fish House.

"Look!" Gabriel said. He pointed toward the roof of the restaurant.

Perched on the edge were two white doves—one for Luca and one for Christi.

I was immediately reminded of the dove release at the cemetery—how fourteen doves traditionally flew off into the sky, but one dove remained perched on top of the mausoleum wall until Luca's casket was placed inside it, something the dove trainer had never seen before in his life. This moment was just what our family needed to feel like God was with us and was using His creation to encourage us.

On Luca's casket, we had his angelic face etched into the bronze next to James 1:12 (ESV), a verse we felt perfectly described Luca: "Blessed is the man who remains steadfast under trial, for when he has stood the test, he will receive the crown of life, which God has promised to those who love him."

Some of the most difficult tests in life are when we're blindsided by the valley (trauma), when we must venture through the treacherous nature of the valley (the fight), or when we're forced to let go on the other side of the fight (grief and loss). I hope that our angelic boy and the lessons he taught us has inspired you in some way to "keep going" through it all—to find courage, to persevere, to accept your life as it is, to abide in Christ along the way, to be animated by joy, to dare to hope, and to, above all else, love like Christ has loved us so that you might receive the crown of life.

Also etched on Luca's tombstone is this phrase:

Forever in Our Hearts, Until We Meet Again

The next time you see a dove, I hope you will think of your loved ones who have gone before you. We all have different backgrounds, but each of us has been uniquely impacted by a loving person in some way or another, whether it was a parent, coach, friend, mentor, or, in our case, our son—an angelic child with special needs who valiantly fought cancer three times.

Our loved ones live on through each of us, until we meet them again. Through trauma, through the fight, through grief and loss, through the valley, do one thing: keep going. Keep going for God. Keep going for them.

Luca passed away on June 21, traditionally the longest day of the year in the Northern Hemisphere, meaning the day with the longest light.

In a way, God's timing seems so appropriate. Luca was a light to everyone who knew him, and now, by telling his story, his light has been shared. From now until we draw our final breaths, June 21 will always remain a significant and solemn day.

We will never forget Luca or the light he left behind. We hope you will think of him, as well as anyone else who showed you light in the darkness of life, especially whenever June 21 rolls around. We hope you remember that their light shines on through you.

Acknowledgments

Thank you to my husband Frank for your unshakeable love and guidance as we journey together through the most impossible circumstances, and to my children, Grace and Gabriel, for giving me countless reasons to keep moving forward. I love each of you more than you'll ever know.

Mom and Dad, I'm beyond grateful to you both for instilling in me a faith in Jesus that provides the kind of hope nothing in this world can destroy. I will carry it with me all my days.

Thank you, Stephen Copeland, for your tireless efforts and insight, and for coming alongside me and playing a vital role in making this book a reality. Also, thank you to Mike Yorkey and David Chong for your incredibly valuable input and edits.

I'm grateful to Dr. David Jeremiah and Dr. John Crawford for penning the afterword and for the love and care you showed our sweet Luca. To everyone who prayed and encouraged me through the writing process, I owe you my deepest gratitude: Lea, Colleen, Debbie, Dave, Debra, Kate, Bettie, Leisha, Summer and Kathe.

Afterword

By Dr. John Crawford
Neuro-Oncologist at Rady Children's Hospital

In the last decade, I've come alongside more than eight hundred families after I've shared the devastating news that their son or daughter has pediatric cancer.

Every family has been special to me. I can't imagine a worse nightmare than being told by a neuro-oncologist such as myself that your child has a life-threatening disease, but there's something extraordinary that happens to families when they go through this journey together, especially if it's done right.

If you're reading this because you have a child or loved one with pediatric cancer, I want you to know that every diagnosis is new, and every outcome is different. There is no single answer, no single cure, or no single path that you have to take. While I know that every cancer diagnosis is incredibly difficult to deal with, I want to remind you that there are different journeys for everyone. It's not always going to be chemotherapy and radiation; there might be alternative therapies. Who am I to tell families where to go? All I can do is educate, and I've found that families almost always make the best decisions for their children.

I once had a young patient with intrinsic pontine glioma (DIPG), which has a survival rate of 10 percent over two years. The family decided to do radiation, but that was it. They would enjoy every single minute with their child with an attitude that this was going to be a celebration from diagnosis until the end. The path they chose worked for their family and resulted in no regrets afterward, and that was incredibly beautiful.

We know that we're born, and we know we're going to die. Everything in between is what we call life. Luca's story reminds us that life is really about hope and faith, and everything happens for a reason along the way. I've found that life is a collision of people, like molecules, but is it really random? I don't think so. I think we all bounce off each other for a reason, and I'm grateful that my path crossed with the Giordano family.

If you were to talk to families who have gone on before you, they would tell you that there is always hope, which is how Frank and Elena chose to travel during their journey with their dear son Luca. They are an example of extraordinary parents who remained upright when their world turned upside down and looked to God for hope and strength. Looking back, I would say they did everything they could, and they did everything right. Even though we weren't able to save their son's life, they are to be commended for their transparency in sharing their pilgrimage into pain in *Luca's Light*. This is a powerful book because they held nothing back and shared the depths of their souls.

What Frank and Elena went through was a tragic voyage filled with heartache, tears, and trepidation. They walked every step of the way with Luca until his final moment on Earth, but think of what they received. Their son taught them and everyone around him the essence of love and the reality of life in a world where every breath, every smell, and every taste must be treasured.

That's the legacy of Luca Joseph Giordano.

I've been doing neuro-oncology for a long time, and I've learned that my profession is much more than prescribing medicine and overseeing chemotherapy and radiation treatments. My job is to be there for families, maintain an attitude of hopefulness, be a shoulder to cry on, and tell them we'll get through this together. I've learned that you never tell a family, "There's no chance." The minute you give up hope for kids and families, they're going to find someone else, and rightly so. Even if the prognosis seems hopeless, I'm never going to give up on the patient and the family.

One thing I've seen, though, is the guilt that consumes many families. I can't tell you the number of times I've started one of my meetings with parents by saying, "I just want you to know that this is not your fault."

Parents wonder if they passed along a bad gene or neglected warning signs, such as the child complaining that his head hurts. Some wonder if the environment was responsible for their child's cancer diagnosis. Was it the food she ate, the air she breathed, the water she drank, or the viruses she was exposed to that caused her pediatric cancer? Was their house too close to power lines? Did they live too close to the freeway? Was there radon in the dirt? Should they have let their soccer-playing daughter head the ball into the net? Many parents think tumors are congenital because they are pediatric, but that's rarely the case.

We don't have good answers yet as to why pediatric brain tumors happen. This is why I echo the Giordanos' call for more research dollars for pediatric cancer because cancer is the number-one cause of death by disease among children. Since 1980, fewer than ten drugs have been developed for use in children with cancer, according to the National Pediatric Cancer Foundation. Only three drugs have been approved for use in children. We need to do more.

While pediatric cancer is a rarity, occurring once in around every three hundred births, if you're the parent of a child with a cancer diagnosis like Luca, the extremely low odds don't matter. You will do anything in your power to help your child survive and live a normal life. This noble quest is why I love coming alongside fathers and mothers to defeat this deadly foe.

I have to let you in on a little secret about being a neuro-oncologist, and it's that we expect failure. I don't like to dwell on it, but our bar is set a little bit lower because we treat a very vulnerable patient population. Sure, we celebrate our successes, but in my field, I walk on pins and needles every day while remaining cautiously optimistic.

I knew there could be no deceit with Frank and Elena. I had to tell it how it was. I couldn't hold anything back, and because I didn't and because Frank and Elena were great people with a deep reservoir of faith, we formed a lasting bond. We trusted each other, which is another reason they are special people.

I always say that the hardest part of my job is giving families bad news. There's shock, a release of tears, and the gushing forth of emotions. What's even worse is telling parents the tumor has come back, like I had to do with Frank and Elena.

Then we embark on a treatment plan. Sometimes we're able to arrest the cancer and move into remission, but all too often, we don't get the results we want. When that happens, some of my most meaningful moments have been with families with a son or daughter at the end of life, when I see families complete their journey from grieving to acceptance to celebration.

I witnessed how that happened with Frank and Elena during Luca's final days. When Frank called me with the news that Luca had passed, I felt for him and the Giordano family and appreciated their unflinching faith that God was in control.

I've changed my philosophy about funerals over the years. I used to think that the memorial service should be a private time for the families to grieve, but these days I make it a point to be there, not only for the closure I think I can offer, but because I've found that I enter into a new relationship with the family after the passing of their son or daughter.

On the morning of Luca's celebration-of-life ceremony, I told the mourners at Shadow Mountain Church that I still remembered the day I met the family in 2009. "What amazing blue eyes and a big smile Luca had," I said. "The first thing I thought was, *I'm going to be in trouble with this one.*"

I said that because Luca was such a special kid. He had a unique quality in the way he interacted with adults, which was full of naiveté and innocence. I couldn't help but be drawn to him, just as my colleagues were at Rady's. Now that he has completed the race, I believe he's on the other side, in a wonderful place called heaven.

He's there right now, looking down on us, sharing his light.

Afterword

By Dr. David Jeremiah
Senior Pastor, Shadow Mountain Community Church

Cancer is personal to me.

I've had two life-threatening bouts with cancer, and I'm grateful that I'm alive to talk about both of them. The first occurrence happened in 1994 when, at the age of fifty-three, I underwent my annual physical examination at the Center for Executive Health in La Jolla, a forty-minute drive from my home in El Cajon.

I thought I was in rather decent shape for a gray-haired guy: I'd knocked off three sermons at Shadow Mountain the day before and was keeping up with pastoral duties, as well as my *Turning Point* radio ministry. In my spare time, I authored several books that explained God's truth.

And then, while I was lying face up on the examination table, my doctor probed the left side of my abdomen—and kept working his fingers. A look of concern knitted his brow.

"Dr. Jeremiah," he said, "you have a mass somewhere in here. Your spleen could be enlarged, so we need to do a CT scan."

A scan was ordered up, and afterward, I was told I'd hear the results the following day. Hearing news like that can work on your mind.

I wonder if there's something wrong.

Does a mass mean a tumor?

And if it's a tumor, is it cancerous or benign?

Those thoughts rattled around my brain the entire drive back to El Cajon. When I stepped through the front door of our home, I didn't mention the CT scan to my wife, Donna, however. No reason to upset her if the results came back negative. Plus, she was leaving in the morning to visit her mom in New Hampshire, so I didn't want to trouble her on the eve of a big trip.

After driving Donna to the airport, I returned to my office, waiting for the phone call from my doctor. When the call finally came in that afternoon, my physician dispensed with the preliminaries. "We found a mass on the spleen," he said. "I had three radiologists examine the scan, and they all believe you have lymphoma, a cancer of the lymphatic system."

The stunning news sent me on an emotional roller-coaster that led to a major surgery to remove the mass. What surgeons basically did was cut me from stem to stern to get at the growth. Their skilled hands kept me alive, but I was told afterward that I would need chemotherapy in the coming months.

Following chemo treatments, I resumed a "normal" life and was exceedingly appreciative that I could continue all my activities on the Lord's behalf. I thought I was doing great until four years later, in 1998, when lymphoma made a comeback in my body. This time, I was told that I had stage IV lymphoma—the absolute worst kind.

Once again, my family and I, along with an army of believers, lifted me in prayer and beseeched God to save my life. Another round of chemotherapy and a stem-cell transplant started me on the road to recovery a second time.

So when Ray Benton informed me that we had a teenage boy with a dire cancer prognosis, I was immediately concerned and asked Ray for the boy's name.

"Luca Giordano," he replied.

I remembered that name—it was so Italian. I recalled how Luca had been hit with brain cancer when he was two, which he and his parents fought valiantly until he miraculously went into remission four years later. Frank and Elena were obviously willing to try everything they could, medically speaking, to keep him alive. Now, in *Luca's Light*, I commend them for sharing their souls and their deepest thoughts about their son's journey.

But despite their heroic efforts, despite the prayers of thousands in our church family as well around the world, Luca Joseph Giordano left us on June 21, 2017.

So what can we take away from his death?

I've met with an incredible number of families over the years who have gone through storms like the Giordanos did, and I've faced them myself, as I've just described. Perhaps a storm is raging around you at this very moment. Perhaps you have a very sick child or a family member with a grim cancer outlook. Perhaps you're facing a mountain of debt or dealing with some other type of difficult situation.

Wherever you are, whatever your crisis may be, there is an important principle at work, and it's this: when you feel helpless, then know that you've become eligible for the assistance of God. You only need to cry out for His salvation, and when you do that, you become a new creature—wiser, stronger, and ready to serve Him. I urge you to run into His waiting arms because that's what He most desires. He is your refuge when all seems lost or a loved one dies. Remember that He is a very present help when all seems lost or hopeless.

Our God is sufficient. Our God is in control. He holds the destiny of the galaxies in His hands—the same heavens that give us a glimpse into how incredibly mighty He is. God tells us in His Word that He loves each and every one of us. He will never run away from you, so you must never run away from Him—especially when times are incredibly difficult, mentally taxing, or extremely sad, as was the case for Frank and Elena.

If I were to die today, I know I would have the thrill of being immediately in the presence of my precious Lord. But having won the good fight against cancer—at least for the moment—I realize I'm benefiting from the considerable consolation of living for Christ in this wonderful world. I'm able to enjoy my loving wife, Donna; counsel my children in adulthood; and see how God nurtures and develops my grandkids.

So what will it be—death or life? I agree with the apostle Paul that it's a win–win proposition, and I dare say that Luca would agree with me at this moment. Whatever happens in our futures, we have so much to be thankful for because we have God. He is everything for me, as I hope He is for you. He has prepared a mansion for all of us, and that's where we will see loved ones and wonderful persons like Luca Giordano.

Someday, we are going to know joy as it is meant to be known and pleasure as we have never known it. That's the legacy that Luca and his light have left us.